New Directions for
Teaching and Learning

Catherine M. Wehlburg
EDITOR-IN-CHIEF

Inquiry-Guided Learning

Virginia S. Lee
EDITOR

Number 129 • Spring 2012
Jossey-Bass
San Francisco

INQUIRY-GUIDED LEARNING
Virginia S. Lee (ed.)
New Directions for Teaching and Learning, no. 129
Catherine M. Wehlburg, Editor-in-Chief

Microfilm copies of issues and articles are available in 16mm and 35mm, as well as microfiche in 105mm, through University Microfilms, Inc., 300 North Zeeb Road, Ann Arbor, MI 48106-1346.

NEW DIRECTIONS FOR TEACHING AND LEARNING (ISSN 0271-0633, electronic ISSN 1536-0768) is part of The Jossey-Bass Higher and Adult Education Series and is published quarterly by Wiley Subscription Services, Inc., A Wiley Company, at Jossey-Bass, One Montgomery Street, Suite 1200, San Francisco, CA 94104-4594. Periodicals postage paid at San Francisco, CA, and at additional mailing offices. POSTMASTER: Send address changes to New Directions for Teaching and Learning, Jossey-Bass, One Montgomery Street, Suite 1200, San Francisco, CA 94104-4594.

New Directions for Teaching and Learning is indexed in CIJE: Current Index to Journals in Education (ERIC), Contents Pages in Education (T&F), Current Abstracts (EBSCO), Educational Research Abstracts Online (T&F), ERIC Database (Education Resources Information Center), Higher Education Abstracts (Claremont Graduate University), and SCOPUS (Elsevier).

SUBSCRIPTIONS cost $89 for individuals and $275 for institutions, agencies, and libraries in the United States. Prices subject to change.

EDITORIAL CORRESPONDENCE should be sent to the editor-in-chief, Catherine M. Wehlburg, c.wehlburg@tcu.edu.

www.josseybass.com

Contents

FROM THE SERIES EDITOR

About This Publication

Since 1980, *New Directions for Teaching and Learning (NDTL)* has brought a unique blend of theory, research, and practice to leaders in postsecondary education. *NDTL* sourcebooks strive not only for solid substance, but also for timeliness, compactness, and accessibility.

The series has four goals: to inform readers about current and future directions in teaching and learning in postsecondary education, to illuminate the context that shapes these new directions, to illustrate these new directions through examples from real settings, and to propose ways in which these new directions can be incorporated into still other settings.

This publication reflects the view that teaching deserves respect as a high form of scholarship. We believe that significant scholarship is conducted not only by researchers who report results of empirical investigations, but also by practitioners who share disciplinary reflections about teaching. Contributors to *NDTL* approach questions of teaching and learning as seriously as they approach substantive questions in their own disciplines, and they deal not only with pedagogical issues but also with the intellectual and social context in which these issues arise. Authors deal on the one hand with theory and research and on the other with practice, and they translate from research and theory to practice and back again.

About This Volume

Inquiry-guided learning is often used as a phrase, but it may be that many of those in higher education do not truly understand what it is and how it can be implemented. This volume provides a deep look at inquiry-guided learning and how it can be a bridge between the traditional classroom experience and the undergraduate research process. By placing inquiry-guided learning in the context of historical approaches to learning, the volume addresses how several institutions have used the process to better educate students.

Catherine M. Wehlburg
Editor-in-Chief

CATHERINE M. WEHLBURG is the assistant provost for institutional effectiveness at Texas Christian University.

PREFACE

The power of inquiry as a way of learning has had widespread appeal in the United States, Canada, the United Kingdom, New Zealand, and Australia. In the United States the publication of the 1998 Boyer Commission report, *Reinventing Undergraduate Education: A Blueprint for America's Research Universities*, heightened interest in inquiry-guided learning (IGL), particularly in research universities.

The report provided inspiration for institutions outside the United States as well: the idea of the teaching and research nexus—that is, forging explicit connections between teaching and research—has caught hold in the United Kingdom, Australia, New Zealand, and Canada. In fact, in some of these countries federal mandates exist to strengthen the links between teaching and research in institutions with a strong research component, and significant resources exist to understand and strengthen the link. Centralized support has also stimulated an active research agenda on the teaching and research nexus among a group of senior scholars in these countries.

Although IGL has an undeniable appeal for colleges and universities that value inquiry implicitly, many institutions adopt IGL, whether in first-year seminars, capstone courses, or points in between, even as they are struggling to understand what it is. Unlike popular teaching strategies such as team-based learning or cooperative learning, IGL comprises a suite of teaching strategies and defies definition as a single heuristic, a prescribed set of practices, or a formula for classroom practice.

In addition, the appeal of IGL has extended beyond research universities to comprehensive universities, liberal arts colleges, and even institutions with a focus on professional studies. There are many reasons for the broader adoption of IGL: its compatibility with constructivism and recent research on learning in a variety of fields, its ability to promote desirable student learning outcomes valued by proponents of both liberal and professional education, and a means to enhance the intellectual culture on campuses striving to strengthen their research mission.

My own interest in IGL began twelve years ago. As the first associate director of the Faculty Center for Teaching and Learning at North Carolina State University (NC State), one of my responsibilities was leadership of a growing, campus-wide IGL initiative. Over time, at NC State and as an

New Directions for Teaching and Learning, no. 129, Spring 2012 © Wiley Periodicals, Inc.
Published online in Wiley Online Library (wileyonlinelibrary.com) • DOI: 10.1002/tl.20001

independent consultant, I found that IGL provided a valuable window into the dynamics of educational reform in higher education. Sitting on the cusp of the teaching and research missions of universities, IGL forces faculty members, staff, and administrators to think about inquiry as a site for learning rather than research and scholarship. Taken seriously, that shift in perspective can be transformational, but not without confronting many guises of institutional and individual inertia to keep things as they already are.

This volume provides a window into the dynamics of undergraduate education reform using IGL. It includes eight institutional case studies bracketed by opening and closing chapters written by me. Although researchers and practitioners at several institutions in this volume have published extensively on their work, to my knowledge there is no single volume that has brought together the experience of institutions in Canada, New Zealand, the United Kingdom, and the United States that have attempted reform through IGL.

Chapter One addresses the necessary question of what IGL actually is: we grappled with this question at NC State as did all of the institutions represented in this volume. The chapter brings together the variety of definitions, conceptual frameworks, models, and rubrics that have been developed to describe inquiry as a way of learning. Chapter Ten reviews the eight case studies in the volume and extracts common themes as well as distinctive aspects of implementation of IGL among them.

Chapters Two through Nine comprise the eight institutional case studies, beginning with The University of Sheffield (TUOS) and ending with McMaster University. The former does an excellent job of laying out broad themes in the context of TUOS that also recur across the other institutional chapters; the latter describes particularly well the tensions between enablers of and challenges to institution-wide transformation through IGL over McMaster's 30-year history with problem- and inquiry-based learning. Chapter Three highlights the importance of conceptualizing IGL as a necessary stage of wider implementation in the context of the University of Gloucestershire.

The remaining institutional case studies describe implementation of IGL at various points in the undergraduate curriculum and in a variety of institutions. Chapters Five and Six describe two very different initiatives to introduce IGL into courses for first-year students: the former, a one-credit seminar at a small, Methodist-affiliated liberal arts college with co-curricular and information literacy components; the latter, high enrollment gateway courses at a public, comprehensive university. Chapters Seven and Eight present institution-wide initiatives at a midsized, Catholic independent university and a research-extensive, land-grant university, respectively.

As a whole the volume provides a succinct and valuable resource for institutions contemplating or in the process of undergraduate reform

NEW DIRECTIONS FOR TEACHING AND LEARNING • DOI: 10.1002/tl

through IGL, for practitioners and scholars of IGL, for instructors seeking good texts for courses on higher education administration, and for administrators seeking to understand the dynamics of and lead undergraduate education reform.

Virginia S. Lee
Editor

VIRGINIA S. LEE is principal and senior consultant of Virginia S. Lee & Associates, LLC, a consulting firm specializing in teaching, learning, assessment, and educational development in higher education. She is a former president (2007–2010) of the Professional and Organizational Development Network in Higher Education, the largest professional organization for educational development specialists in the United States.

1

Inquiry-guided learning has widespread appeal for a variety of institutions of higher education throughout the world. As a suite of teaching strategies that defies a simple prescription for practice, inquiry-guided learning challenges practitioners to develop conceptual frameworks that describe inquiry as a site of student learning rather than of traditional scholarship.

What Is Inquiry-Guided Learning?

Virginia S. Lee

The power of inquiry as a way of learning has had widespread appeal in the United States, Canada, the United Kingdom, New Zealand, and Australia. In the United States the publication of the 1998 Boyer Commission report, *Reinventing Undergraduate Education: A Blueprint for America's Research Universities* (Boyer Commission on Educating Undergraduates in the Research University, 1998), heightened interest in inquiry-guided learning (IGL), particularly in research universities. Using inquiry as a mode of learning capitalizes on the strength of the faculty in research, the report argued: inquiry is part of the distinctive ecology of the research university in which faculty, graduate students, and undergraduate students should all participate.

The report provided inspiration for institutions outside the United States as well: the idea of the teaching and research nexus—that is, forging explicit connections between teaching and research—has caught hold in the United Kingdom, Australia, New Zealand, and Canada. In fact, in some of these countries federal mandates and significant resources exist to strengthen the links between teaching and research in institutions with a strong research component. Centralized support has also stimulated an active research agenda on the teaching and research nexus among a group of senior scholars in these countries (for example, Brew, 2003; Barnett, 2005; Spronken-Smith and Walker, 2010).

In addition, the appeal of IGL has extended beyond research universities to comprehensive universities, liberal arts colleges, and even institutions with a focus on professional studies. There are many reasons for the

New Directions for Teaching and Learning, no. 129, Spring 2012 © Wiley Periodicals, Inc.
Published online in Wiley Online Library (wileyonlinelibrary.com) • DOI: 10.1002/tl.20002

broader adoption of IGL. From a theoretical standpoint, IGL is compatible with constructivism and research from psychology, education, and neuroscience on the dynamics of learning and its implications for educational practice that have gained greater credibility over the past ten to fifteen years. In recent years learning outcomes have become the recommended, if not widely accepted, starting point for planning courses and curricula and, coupled with assessment, ensuring accountability in higher education. Regardless of institutional type, most colleges and universities identify over and over certain outcomes, including critical thinking, problem solving, taking responsibility for one's own learning, and the desire for lifelong learning, as being particularly important. IGL promotes these kinds of outcomes and the specific skills associated with them, for example, the ability to ask good questions, to analyze and interpret evidence, and to select and justify the best solution to a problem (Lee, 2011).

Further, IGL develops abilities and attitudes valued by proponents of both liberal and professional education and by those who feel that higher education should equip students for the varied demands of modern life including the requirements of the workplace. As students become increasingly skilled at organizing an inquiry or tackling a complex problem or issue with other people, they develop a set of capacities and attitudes relevant to work, home, and community (Lee, 2011). On a more philosophical level, through IGL students become increasingly comfortable with and able to make good decisions and judgments under conditions of uncertainty, a hallmark of intellectual growth and maturity.

Finally, the research university has become the aspirational model for many institutions of higher education whose previous focus was primarily teaching. As these institutions increase the expectations for their faculty to conduct research, they may also adopt IGL as a way to bridge the teaching and newly emphasized research missions of the institution and to enhance the intellectual culture on campus. In this volume the reader will find examples from a range of institutions: research and comprehensive universities, liberal arts colleges including those with a religious affiliation, and a university with an emphasis on professional programs.

What Is Inquiry-Guided Learning?

IGL promotes the acquisition of new knowledge, abilities, and attitudes through students' increasingly independent investigation of questions, problems, and issues, for which there often is no single answer (Lee, 2004). As Figure 1.1 illustrates, IGL is a subset of so-called active learning strategies that also belongs to a group of strategies known as inductive teaching and learning methods (Prince and Felder, 2006). Problem-based learning is a specific type of IGL that arose in fields such as medicine and engineering in which problem solving is a dominant mode of

Figure 1.1. Inquiry-Guided Learning as a Subset of Active Learning

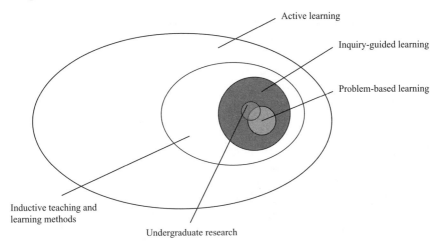

inquiry. Undergraduate research, properly structured, is also a type of IGL.

Implementing Inquiry-Guided Learning

Although IGL has an undeniable appeal for colleges and universities that value inquiry implicitly, many institutions adopt IGL, whether in first-year seminars, capstone courses, or points in between, even as they are struggling to understand what it is. Unlike popular teaching strategies such as team-based learning or cooperative learning, IGL comprises a suite of teaching strategies and defies definition as a single heuristic, a prescribed set of practices, or a formula for classroom practice. Frequently, the elusiveness of IGL is a frustration for faculty who want to know precisely what it is and how to implement it in their courses, which in turn can be an obstacle to its widespread adoption. Very broadly, IGL requires faculty members to reimagine their discipline as a framework for learning (Riordan and Roth, 2005) rather than a framework for scholarship. This is a very tall order, particularly in view of the inadequate preparation for teaching during graduate study and the recalcitrance of the conceptualization of teaching and learning as content delivery and memorization, respectively.

   In the eight institutions represented in this volume, readers will note the wealth of antecedents drawn upon and models and mechanisms created to delimit IGL sufficiently for implementation. For example, McMaster University, an early pioneer in inquiry-guided learning as problem-based learning, drew originally on Bell's (1966) thinking on the reform of general education and the work of Knowles (1975) and Candy (1991) on self-directed learning. Other antecedents include Kolb's (1984) experiential learning cycle as a general model of inquiry and various representations of critical thinking, a cousin of inquiry.

The development of inquiry models has been particularly active in Canada, the United Kingdom, Australia, and New Zealand, although there are examples of models generated in the United States. Possible reasons for the heightened activity include the greater emphasis on the scholarship of educational practice in those countries; federal mandates regarding the teaching-research nexus; the funding of national centers as hubs of practice and research on IGL; and the resulting number of researchers, some of them quite senior, who have made IGL a central focus of their research agenda.

The overwhelming challenge in model development is devising a single scheme that represents accurately and credibly the diverse processes of inquiry in the sciences, mathematics, humanities, social sciences, fine arts, and professional programs. Models that have wide application, such as Kolb's experiential cycle, may have little utility as instructional heuristics for a majority of faculty members, who seek greater explicit guidance within their discipline. Models that offer explicit guidance within a specific discipline or set of disciplines such as the sciences may have little perceived relevance for practitioners in other fields. Added to the challenge of model creation is the developmental aspect of IGL—that is, the degree to which students are able to engage in independent inquiry, how much guidance is permissible in IGL, and how to characterize or represent guidance at successive stages of student development toward independent inquiry.

Consequently, the models represented in this volume and elsewhere variously describe the process of inquiry itself, the progression from guided to independent inquiry, the instructional implications of IGL, or a combination. Not surprisingly, the scientific process (or its adaptation to the social sciences) is the inspiration for most of these models. Models that describe the process of inquiry (for example, Hudspith and Jenkins, 2001; Justice and others, 2007) typically account for most of the following stages of inquiry: exploration, question or problem identification, inquiry design including methods of investigation, collection and analysis of data or evidence, development of conclusions or solutions, and communication of results. An interesting early model, Gowin's Vee heuristic for understanding knowledge (Novak and Gowin, 1984), takes a different, epistemological approach: it attempts to deconstruct and make transparent the process of knowledge formation itself, particularly in the sciences, and thereby address directly students' misconception of knowledge as a reservoir of facts rather than a process.

Another set of models addresses the developmental implications of IGL: specifically, the nature and degree of guidance at successive stages of student development toward independent inquiry and expectations regarding student performance of the various stages of the inquiry process at each developmental stage. For example, Bonnstetter (1998) describes an inquiry continuum that progresses from "traditional hands on" inquiry in which the teacher controls all stages of the process of inquiry, through structured, guided, student-directed, and finally independent student-research inquiry. From two dimensions, tutor- or client-framed versus student-framed inquiry and exploring existing versus building new knowledge, Levy (forthcoming) derives four modes of inquiry—Identifying, Pursuing, Producing, and Authoring. Beginning with tutor- or client-framed inquiry that explores existing knowledge, the modes progress to student-framed inquiry that builds new knowledge.

Models that describe expectations regarding student performance of the various stages of the inquiry process and the conditions of performance at different developmental levels are essentially developmental rubrics. These frameworks include the Research Skills Development (RSD) Framework (University of Adelaide, 2006) and the Association of American Colleges and Schools (n.d.) Inquiry and Analysis VALUE rubric. For example, the RSD Framework comprises six facets of inquiry and five levels of student autonomy. In Facet E ("Students synthesize and analyze and apply new knowledge"), Level I is "Synthesize and analyze information/data to reproduce existing knowledge to prescribed formats. Ask questions of clarification and curiosity" and Level V is "Synthesize, analyze, and apply information/data to fill self-identified gaps or extend knowledge."

How institutions and instructors actually use these models as they integrate IGL into courses and the curriculum is another matter. As I noted earlier, the models, in whatever form, bring necessary conceptual clarity to the term IGL: for researchers, including assessment specialists, the development of models is both an end in itself and an essential tool for analyzing patterns of implementation and student performance in courses, across the curriculum, and between institutions; for instructors the models are suggestive of pedagogical practice at various developmental levels; and for institutions as a whole, a compelling model contributes to a common language about IGL.

Although they are suggestive of classroom practice, the models do not provide explicit guidance on specific learning activities and experiences. For example, in one of Levy's four modes of inquiry, producing, "students explore open questions, problems, scenarios, or lines of inquiry, framed by teachers or others such as an external 'client' in interaction with a knowledge base." An instructor might well ask: How? What kinds of open questions, problems, or scenarios? How does the knowledge base come into play? How do I present it? and so on. Similarly at Level II of Facet E of the RSD Framework students "organize information/data using a recommended structure and process": What data? Where do they come from? What recommended structure and process? How and when does the instructor introduce it? and so on. Often instructors who are comfortable with traditional teaching that emphasizes the lecture want guidance of this kind.

Consequently, another, less common approach to the creation of models for IGL acknowledges the developmental level of instructors rather than students. For example, Lee (2011) created a developmental rubric on the use of IGL that reflects the varied conceptualizations of teaching that instructors hold (see Exhibit 1.1). The rubric recognizes that how instructors implement IGL depends as much on their own frequently unexamined assumptions about teaching as their instructional response to the developmental level of their students. So an instructor who sees himself as a presenter of knowledge and trusts primarily his own control over knowledge delivery will implement IGL quite differently from an instructor who sees herself as a collaborator with students in the process of inquiry and trusts the process of inquiry itself as a force in learning regardless of the level of the students. As a supplement to the rubric, Lee (2011) also provided selected semester patterns in IGL courses that may loosely correspond to the stages in the developmental rubric (see Table 1.1). So instructors at the Experimenting stage may use patterns 1 and 2, Pseudo- and Emerging-IGL, when implementing IGL; at the Developing stage, patterns 3–6; and at the Committed stage, patterns 6 and 7. Some readers may argue that semester patterns 3–6 also correspond to student developmental levels: that is, less instructor guidance toward independent inquiry as students progress through the curriculum. The semester patterns also offer instructors more pedagogical guidance on how to implement IGL, while still falling short of absolute prescription.

Model development notwithstanding, readers will observe a common finding regarding implementation in the eight institutional examples in this volume: the importance of instructor and program discretion in the interpretation and implementation of IGL. It is indeed a paradox of educational development that as much as instructors ask for explicit guidance on the implementation of IGL, they also require flexibility in how they ultimately interpret and incorporate it into their courses. Further, the paradox holds regardless of institutional type or country. Possible reasons for the requirement of flexibility include the importance of the value of autonomy in the academy and, as noted earlier, the distinctive cultures and methods of inquiry of the academic disciplines and the varied conceptualizations of teaching and learning held by instructors.

Instead of the conceptual clarity afforded by models, over time many institutions develop a broad, common understanding of IGL that guides implementation across the institution. The common understanding frequently takes the form of a consensus definition or a set of student learning outcomes. In my own experience at North Carolina State University, four broad student learning outcomes—taking responsibility for one's own learning, critical thinking, developing habits of independent inquiry, and intellectual growth and maturity—as well as a common definition of IGL

Exhibit 1.1. Holistic Developmental Rubric on the Use of Inquiry-Guided Learning by Instructors

Committed

Inquiry is the dominant mode of learning and the primary stimulus for knowledge acquisition.

Seamless development of the skills of inquiry and the acquisition of knowledge through the process of inquiry itself.

Skillful, and often invisible, balance of challenge and support in ways appropriate to the developmental level of students; enables students to function with a high degree of independence.

Primary source of trust is in the process of inquiry as a mode of learning and the outcomes and products of inquiry as credible or valid assessment.

Instructor exhibits a tolerance for uncertainty in the inquiry process and openness to unexpected directions set by students.

Instructor functions chiefly as a collaborator with students in the process of inquiry.

Developing

Inquiry as a mode of learning but often after explicit preparation of students using more traditional instructional methods.

Separate development of the skills of inquiry and the acquisition of knowledge through explicit instruction.

Balance of challenge and support in ways appropriate to the developmental level of students; mechanisms of support are visible.

Primary source of trust is in the guidance of the instructor with guidance taking a variety of forms.

Instructor exhibits some tolerance for uncertainty within anticipated boundaries of student performance.

Instructor functions chiefly as a guide to students during the process of inquiry.

Experimenting

Some inquiry as a mode of assessment but only after explicit preparation of students using traditional instructional methods.

Acquisition of knowledge through explicit instruction with some experimentation engaging students in the skills of inquiry through isolated learning activities.

Primary source of trust is in instructor control over knowledge delivery.

Instructor exhibits little tolerance for uncertainty beyond isolated and carefully controlled opportunities for student engagement.

Instructor functions chiefly as an organizer and presenter of knowledge.

Source: Lee, 2011.

Table 1.1. Selected Semester Patterns in an Inquiry-Guided Learning Course

Type	No.	Pattern	Comments
Pseudo-IGL	1	K, K, K, K, K, K, I	A very traditional course with a final inquiry-like project, often a research paper for which students have not been prepared.
Emerging IGL	2	K, i1, K, K, K, i2, K, K, i3	Instructor experimentation with inquiry by introducing inquiry exercises as in-class activities or assignments.
Guided Inquiry	3	K, i1, i2, I, K, i3, i4, I . . .	A series of units each built around an inquiry experience, structured by the instructor, for which students have been prepared through presentation of relevant content and inquiry skills development.
	4	K, K, K, i1, i2, i3, I	A final inquiry experience, perhaps with some opportunity for student choice and design, for which students have been prepared through presentation of relevant content and inquiry skills development.
	5	Ia, Ib, Ic, Id, Ie, I	The course as a series of feeder assignments, designed by the instructor and on which students receive feedback, leading up to a final inquiry experience.
	6	I, K, i1, i2, I, K, i3, i4 . . .	A series of inquiry experiences, each designed to address a targeted content area and to develop the skills of inquiry. Typical of problem-based learning.
Inquiry	7	I, K, i1, i2, i3, i4 . . .	An inquiry experience, perhaps student designed, through which students acquire content relevant to the inquiry and further develop the skills of inquiry.

Legend: K = presentation of knowledge/content; I = inquiry; Ia = feeder assignment to inquiry; i1 = guided inquiry skill development.

Source: Lee, 2011.

(see Lee, 2004, pp. 9–10) provided just enough conceptual clarity while still permitting many variations in practice. Further, as instructors integrated IGL into courses, they drew upon varied sources of inspiration to guide their practice including course goals and objectives that interpreted the broad outcomes more specifically in the context of their disciplines, alternative models of inquiry and representations of critical thinking, information literacy outcomes, rubrics, compatible teaching strategies, and innovations adopted by other instructors.

Readers will observe a similar pattern across the institutions represented here: a broad, common understanding of IGL with a wealth of variations in practice across the academic disciplines.

Conclusion

IGL appeals to a range of institutions of higher education seeking variously to capitalize on the research expertise of their faculty, bridge their teaching and research missions, further a broad set of desirable student learning outcomes, and enhance the intellectual culture on their campuses. Particularly over the past fifteen years, it has been very much in the air as a compelling approach to learning and adopted widely even as colleges and universities struggle to understand what IGL is. Because IGL comprises a suite of teaching practices that defies a simple prescription for practice, practitioners have developed conceptual frameworks, models, and developmental rubrics as a necessary first step of implementation. Taken together these frameworks, models, and rubrics represent a collective effort to define inquiry as a site of student learning rather than faculty scholarship.

References

Association of American Colleges and Schools. *Inquiry and Analysis VALUE Rubric.* Washington, D.C.: American Association of Colleges and Schools, n.d.. Retrieved June 23, 2011, from http://www.aacu.org/value/rubrics/pdf/InquiryAnalysis.pdf.

Barnett, R., ed. *Reshaping the University: New Relationships between Research, Scholarship and Teaching.* Maidenhead, United Kingdom: McGraw-Hill/Open University Press, 2005.

Bell, D. *The Reforming of General Education.* New York: Columbia University Press, 1966.

Bonnstetter, R. J. "Inquiry: Learning from the Past with an Eye on the Future." *Electronic Journal of Science Education,* 1998, 3(1). Retrieved June 26, 2010, from http://wolfweb.unr.edu/homepage/jcannon/ejse/bonnstetter.html.

Boyer Commission Report on Educating Undergraduates in the Research University. *Reinventing Undergraduate Education: A Blueprint for America's Research Universities.* Stony Brook, NY: Stony Brook University, 1998.

Brew, A. "Teaching and Research: New Relationships and Their Implications for Inquiry-Based Teaching and Learning in Higher Education." *Higher Education Research and Development,* 2003, 22(1), 3–18.

Candy, P. *Self-Direction for Lifelong Learning.* San Francisco: Jossey-Bass, 1991.

Hudspith, B., and H. Jenkins. *Teaching the Art of Inquiry*. Halifax, Nova Scotia, Canada: Society for Teaching and Learning in Higher Education, 2001.

Justice, C., and others. "Inquiry in Higher Education: Reflections and Directions on Course Design and Teaching Methods." *Journal of Innovative Higher Education*, 2007, *31*(4), 201–214.

Knowles, M. *Self-Directed Learning*. Englewood Cliffs, N.J.: Prentice Hall, 1975.

Kolb, D. A. *Experiential Learning: Experience as the Source of Learning and Development*. Englewood Cliffs, N.J.: Prentice Hall, 1984.

Lee, V. S., ed. *Teaching and Learning Through Inquiry: A Guidebook for Institutions and Instructors*. Sterling, Va.: Stylus, 2004.

Lee, V. S. "The Power of Inquiry as a Way of Learning." *Innovative Higher Education*, 2011, *36*(3), 149–160.

Levy, P. "Embedding Inquiry and Research for Knowledge-Building into Mainstream Higher Education: A UK Perspective." *CUR Quarterly*, forthcoming.

Novak, J. D., and D. B. Gowin *Learning How to Learn*. New York: Cambridge University Press, 1984.

Prince, M. J., and R. M. Felder. "Inductive Teaching and Learning Methods: Definitions, Comparisons, and Research Bases." *Journal of Engineering Education*, 2006, *95*(2), 123–138.

Riordan, R., and J. Roth, eds. *Disciplines as Frameworks for Student Learning: Teaching the Practice of the Disciplines*. Sterling, Va.: Stylus, 2005.

Spronken-Smith, R., and R. Walker. "Can Inquiry-based Learning Strengthen the Links between Teaching and Disciplinary Research?" *Studies in Higher Education*, 2010, *35*(6), 723–740.

University of Adelaide. Research Skill Development, 2006. Retrieved June 23, 2011, from http://www.adelaide.edu.au/clpd/rsd/.

VIRGINIA S. LEE is principal and senior consultant of Virginia S. Lee & Associates, LLC (Durham, North Carolina), a consulting firm that specializes in teaching, learning, and assessment in higher education.

NEW DIRECTIONS FOR TEACHING AND LEARNING • DOI: 10.1002/tl

2

*This chapter discusses themes from a five-year institutional develop-
ment program for inquiry-guided learning (IGL) at The University
of Sheffield. It presents a conceptual framework for IGL instructional design, gives examples of IGL courses, and highlights features
of the program's approach to the facilitation of educational change.*

Developing Inquiry-Guided Learning in a Research University in the United Kingdom

Philippa Levy

A number of universities in the United Kingdom (UK) have launched institution-wide initiatives recently to embed inquiry and research more firmly
into the student experience. Among these, the Centre for Inquiry-based
Learning in the Arts and Social Sciences (CILASS) led a five-year development program at The University of Sheffield (TUOS) between 2005 and
2010. CILASS was a national Centre for Excellence in Teaching and
Learning (CETL) awarded to TUOS as part of a government-funded, large-
scale program for university learning and teaching enhancement in England
and Northern Ireland. It was funded to carry out both intra- and interinstitutional development work stemming from existing practice at TUOS in
inquiry-based learning, referred to here as inquiry-guided learning (IGL)
for the sake of consistency with other chapters. The CILASS program, with
objectives that are discussed in more detail by Levy (2007), included
strands on reward and recognition for teaching, curriculum development
and innovation, educational assessment and research, enhancement of the
university's physical estate, and dissemination of good practice. Its main
focus was on IGL in the arts, humanities, and social sciences, but its mission also extended to supporting development in a range of other disciplines. As an operationally independent unit reporting directly to the
university's pro-vice chancellor for learning and teaching, CILASS worked
in close partnership with a wide range of professional services and

NEW DIRECTIONS FOR TEACHING AND LEARNING, no. 129, Spring 2012 © Wiley Periodicals, Inc.
Published online in Wiley Online Library (wileyonlinelibrary.com) • DOI: 10.1002/tl.20003

academic departments at TUOS to promote and further develop IGL collaboratively in the institution.

This chapter offers an overview of some key themes from CILASS's own institutional development work.

Why Inquiry-Guided Learning?

TUOS is a research institution that is committed to providing students with a learning experience shaped by strong, positive interactions between research, learning, and teaching. Active student involvement in inquiry and research, including through IGL, has been identified as an essential aspect of research-led learning and teaching. The institution's formal Learning, Teaching and Assessment Strategy of 2005–2010—the strategic context for the IGL development program—set the objective for students in all disciplines to experience an inquiry-infused approach to learning; subsequent strategic planning reflects the same position. Qualities and skills fostered by inquiry, such as initiative, self-belief, responsibility, independence of mind, critical judgment, creativity, self-management, collaboration, and information literacy, are embedded in the stated attributes of the "Sheffield Graduate," one of which is the capacity for independent learning and research (http://www.shef.ac.uk/sheffieldgraduate). The term *inquiry-based learning* was not in widespread use across TUOS before the IGL development program was launched in 2005. However, IGL approaches—broadly defined—already had been identified as a feature of excellent instructional practice in the institution and fit well with the university's strategic goals for the student learning experience.

In the course of the five-year development program, we were able to explore the student and staff experience in some detail, through assessment of new initiatives and a number of research studies (see, for example, van Oostrum, Steadman-Jones, and Carson, 2007; Cox, Levy, Stordy, and Webber, 2008; Stafford, 2008; Verbaan, 2008; Rossiter, Petrulis, and Biggs, 2010; Webber, 2010). Experiences of the benefits of IGL at TUOS proved to be broadly consistent with those reported in the wider literature, as summarized by Healey and Jenkins (2009). The growing international evidence base confirms that IGL can be a powerful means of encouraging engagement in deep approaches to subject learning.IGL can also foster high-order intellectual, personal, and professional attributes that are especially relevant to life in a complex and challenging world, including those required for democratic citizenship and employment in the knowledge economy. By positioning students as active, critical participants in knowledge production, in partnership with faculty as members of the same scholarly communities, IGL also counters the effects of a market-driven higher education environment that frames students as consumers in the learning process (Levy, Little, and Whelan, 2011). This is not to underplay the challenges that often arise when designing, facilitating, and participating in IGL,

NEW DIRECTIONS FOR TEACHING AND LEARNING • DOI: 10.1002/tl

which encourage students to take a significant amount of responsibility for their own learning and to move toward independence in using the scholarly practices and resources of their disciplines to create and share knowledge. Considerable intellectual and practical challenges can arise from this, for students and faculty alike, not least in unsettling prior educational values and expectations. Nevertheless, IGL development projects at TUOS confirmed the considerable benefits of student learning through inquiry across a wide range of pure and applied disciplines, irrespective of whether they had research careers in mind.

Defining, Conceptualizing, and Designing IGL

There is no one way to conceptualize or implement IGL, and the development program at TUOS did not seek to impose one theory or model on the development of practice. We interpreted IGL as a flexible approach that can take a variety of forms to suit different educational purposes, including fostering the acquisition of clearly defined, "certain" knowledge or, alternatively, engaging students with multiple perspectives and contestation through exploration of open-ended questions to which definitive answers have not yet been reached or do not exist. The view we adopted sees IGL as encompassing related approaches including problem-based learning (PBL). Some faculty drew on PBL protocols to design IGL tasks and processes, whereas others drew more on the pattern of research practice in their discipline. We used the cycle shown in Figure 2.1 to propose a broad IGL framework adaptable to different contexts (see Justice and others, 2007, for an alternative framework).

We learned that successful IGL flows from questioning, purposeful, imaginative engagement with well-designed inquiry tasks in a learning environment that provides an appropriate balance of challenge and support. Instructional design for IGL is process focused rather than content focused even when the intention is to engage students with very specific content along the way in that it is students' engagement with an inquiry process that drives their activity. Sometimes the term IGL is used to refer specifically to teacher-guided investigations of student-framed questions. In contrast, the CILASS program used it to refer also to approaches in which faculty themselves formulate the questions. IGL initiatives supported by CILASS involved both large and small cohorts of students and were richly diverse and often innovative in character. Starting points included intriguing fieldwork or design problems, real-world themes generated by external agencies or arising out of professional practice, complex case scenarios, stimuli such as visual resources, or simply open research questions within the domain. Some examples of IGL at TUOS follow:

- First-year architecture undergraduates create public art for a local urban regeneration initiative.

Figure 2.1. An IGL Cycle

students
communicate and
share results of
their inquiry

students/tutors
establish question,
problem, theme

students reflect,
discuss, critique,
analyze,
conceptualize,
synthesize, create,
receive feedback

students draw on
their existing
knowledge and,
with support,
decide on the
direction and
methods of their
inquiry

students explore
evidence,
interrogate texts,
conduct
experiments, etc.,
interacting with
information via a
range of sources

Source: Levy and others, 2010.

- First-year geography undergraduates learn about statistical methods by exploring an open-ended geographical question for which a quantitative approach offers useful insights.
- First-year information management undergraduates investigate the information needs and practices of users of the 3-D virtual world, Second Life.
- First-year law undergraduates investigate the nature of legal problems and develop legal information skills through inquiry exercises and scenarios in a blended learning setting.
- Second-year English literature undergraduates conduct a multidimensional inquiry into one literary text by experimenting with eight modes of inquiry and interconnections between them.
- Second-year medical undergraduates investigate media responses to methicillin-resistant staphylococcus aureus (MRSA) in historical

perspective, including conducting interviews with journalists and assessing responses to scientific evidence.

- Third-year French literature and culture undergraduates work in groups to explore key themes in French contemporary fine art and assemble a virtual exhibition of artists' work.
- Third-year sociology undergraduates conduct research on issues of social importance for clients such as the Citizens Advice Bureau.
- Master's students in psychology engage with contested domains in cognitive neuroscience by formulating their own questions and conducting student-led inquiry projects.

Over the course of our development program, we clarified and refined our conceptualization of IGL. IGL frequently is seen as a form of active learning in which students carry out research-like activities to explore and master an existing knowledge base. But in some modes it is capable of extending student learning toward and well into the realms of genuine scholarship and research, with potential to result in original intellectual and creative outcomes of importance and value. We moved toward a view of IGL that is inclusive of both of these perspectives. Reflecting this, IGL is defined here as *a cluster of related instructional approaches in which student inquiry or research drives the student experience of learning and participation in knowledge building.* The terms inquiry and research are used together to refer to all forms of scholarly exploration and investigation carried out by students as part of studies in any discipline. Learning and knowledge building signal, respectively, a distinction between individual conceptual change and contribution to improved thinking or knowledge in a domain (Bereiter, 2002).

This conceptualization is illustrated in Figure 2.2, which offers a broad-based framework for instructional design in IGL that builds in part on work by Healey (2005; see also Levy, 2011). It brings to the fore three fundamental instructional design considerations, as identified by CILASS research: the epistemic purposes and orientation of students' inquiry; where primary responsibility lies for establishing the inquiry question or theme; and the level and nature of process support, or scaffolding, provided (that is, the guidance, structure, and resources aimed at helping students to engage productively with the inquiry process). The vertical axis represents epistemic orientation in terms of the distinction between inquiry for learning and for knowledge building. The horizontal axis differentiates between students and faculty (or others) in framing the inquiry question. Process support is represented as a third dimension mapped onto each quadrant. The matrix identifies four ideal modes of IGL at different levels of sophistication labeled, respectively, *Identifying, Pursuing, Producing,* and *Authoring;* all four modes are taken to be equally valuable, depending on educational context and purposes.

The framework allows for different instructional designs on which IGL and PBL may be mapped as well as different approaches to designing

Figure 2.2. Modes of IGL

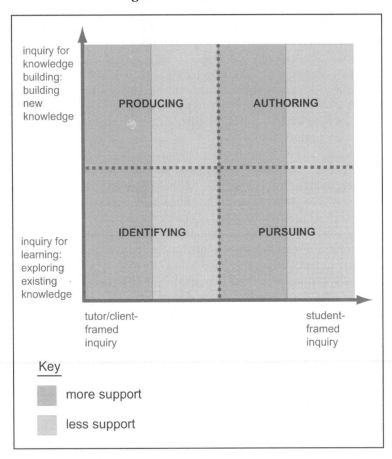

Key

Authoring: Students explore their own open questions, problems, scenarios, or lines of inquiry, in interaction with a knowledge base (How can I answer my open question?).

Producing: Students explore open questions, problems, scenarios, or lines of inquiry, framed by teachers or others such as an external "client," in interaction with a knowledge base (How can I answer this open question?).

Pursuing: Students explore a knowledge base actively by pursuing their own questions, problems, scenarios, or lines of inquiry (What is the existing answer or response to my question?).

Identifying: Students explore a knowledge base actively in response to questions, problems, scenarios, or lines of inquiry framed by teachers (What is the existing answer or response to this question?).

Source: Levy and Petrulis, 2011.

progression in IGL through the levels of study. A number of development projects supported by CILASS were concerned specifically with building IGL more explicitly into the first undergraduate year and with improving structured progression in "the inquiry curriculum" through the levels of study. We found that introducing IGL early could enthuse students and develop self-confidence, as well as allow positive norms relating to IGL to be established (discussed for example, by Cox, Levy, Stordy, and Webber, 2008; Webber, 2010).

Progression in IGL is a broadly sequential process through Identifying, Pursuing, Producing, and Authoring modes culminating in student-framed open inquiry at more advanced levels. Alternatively, it is a spiral process whereby students are introduced to open inquiry (Producing, Authoring) at more introductory levels. Student and staff feedback through our IGL assessment and research studies consistently pointed to the need to provide plenty of process support at less advanced levels of study, for example, in areas relating to information literacy or collaborative working as well as discipline-based inquiry methods. However, an investigation into the first-year student experience suggested that early opportunities to engage in inquiry for knowledge building—that is, in inquiry that is strongly supported but open ended in character—may yield significant educational benefits (Levy and Petrulis, 2012). The findings of this study also suggested that opportunities for first-year students to frame their own inquiry questions may have particularly beneficial effects.

The CILASS program identified information literacy as fundamental to successful inquiry and research practice in all disciplines and, working in close partnership with the university library, adopted a special thematic focus on integrating support for information literacy development explicitly into IGL. We interpreted information literacy as the ability to find and use information effectively in any given context, through any medium whether digital or other, and as encompassing higher-order capabilities such as critical evaluation, synthesis, and ethical judgment as well as technical skills in areas such as information search. An instructional developer role with special expertise in information literacy teaching was created to support this aspect of IGL development, a strategy that led to the development of a wide range of creative information literacy development tasks for IGL courses (see, for example, McKinney, Jones, and Turkington, 2011). Some examples are

- Students construct annotated bibliographies related to their inquiry according to a specified set of instructions.
- Students trace the academic research source of a popular science news item.
- Students search relevant databases for a journal article of interest and write a critical review.
- Students write reflective reviews of their personal information literacy development using prompts derived from a relevant conceptual model.

- Students interview a peer about their information needs for an inquiry project and carry out a literature search on their behalf.
- Students use bookmarking and other Web 2.0 technologies such as wikis to create peer-reviewed, shared information resources for IGL tasks.
- Students research a Wikipedia entry for accuracy and redraft it.

Development Challenges and Strategies

During the course of the IGL development initiative, we encountered a range of change facilitation challenges, not least those caused by the tensions that exist between research and teaching in a research university and by the need for educational development and innovation to compete with faculty's many other commitments and pressures. A further challenge from the outset was to find an accessible, shareable language for conversations about IGL. We worked hard to counteract perceptions that the term *inquiry-guided learning* might simply be jargon for standard educational practice with some element of active or independent learning (for example, students doing lab exercises or library-based reading following lectures and seminars). We learned that in promoting IGL across different academic and professional disciplines, it was important to emphasize the flexibility of the approach. But often there also was a need to emphasize the distinctive character of IGL in terms of the primary role played by the inquiry question and process in the student experience and the instructional design and facilitation implications that stem from that, for example in the sequencing of tasks and in the roles played by faculty in providing guidance and support.

We monitored our development approach throughout the life cycle of the program, using an adaptation of "theory of change" evaluation methodology to assess progress and impact, as discussed by Hart, Diercks-O'Brien, and Powells (2009). Assessment showed that the program made a strong contribution to cultural change at TUOS, not only in developing understanding and practice in IGL and demonstrating very powerful reach in terms of the student experience, but also in developing the institution's approach to the practice of educational enhancement. Following is a summary of some key features of our approach to facilitating educational change for IGL.

Bottom-Up, Top-Down, and Middle-Through. We adopted a strongly participatory model of initial conceptualization and ongoing governance for the change program with its agenda established collaboratively by representatives of a wide range of stakeholder groups among faculty and professional services staff. Faculty members in formal IGL champion roles encouraged the engagement of colleagues and helped disseminate good practice. Close alignment with institutional strategy for learning and teaching created opportunities to influence formal planning and development at institutional and departmental levels. The championing of IGL by senior management and their support for new approaches to change facilitation also proved to be crucial success factors.

Targeted, Multilevel Funding and Support. We designed funding schemes for IGL development projects to stimulate and reward projects at multiple levels of the institution by variously targeting individuals and teams and academic and professional services departments. We set thematic priorities to encourage engagement with key aspects of IGL; these included collaborative inquiry, information literacy development, and the use of new digital technologies. We encouraged creativity, experimentation, and risk taking in innovation. Award of project funding was tolerant of open endedness in early project plans while emphasizing the requirement to assess progress, outcomes, and impact. Instructional designers and researchers supported portfolios of projects and acted proactively as "winged messengers" (Little, 2008) between projects in different parts of the institution and to connect people with shared purposes and interests.

Reward and Recognition. We placed emphasis on promoting enhancement of institutional reward and recognition for teaching through academic staff review and promotions criteria and award schemes. An annual award scheme for excellence in IGL included a student-nominated strand and rewarded individual staff, staff teams, and academic and professional services departments.

Strong Multiprofessional Partnerships. We encouraged multiprofessional partnerships around the IGL theme (including staff from learning and teaching quality and development services, information services, information technology and audiovisual services, estates, and career services as well as faculty) through strategies including internships with the CETL, the establishment of an IGL library liaison role, commissioning of assistance with learning technology and other support for projects, and a range of development events targeted specifically at different professional groups to provide opportunities to explore the implications of IGL from multiple professional perspectives. For example, a tailored program of professional development about IGL for information services staff included rollout to customer services staff as well as librarians in instructional roles.

Strong Student Partnership. Student partnership for educational enhancement was a central feature of our strategy. We set up a student ambassador network for IGL, comprising undergraduate participants from each academic department with which the CETL worked and based on small part-time, paid appointments. The network was cofacilitated by a student on an annual appointment and a member of staff. Student ambassadors organized into working groups and were active as individuals in their own departments. They produced films and other information about IGL including informational Web pages for students and a journal, coordinated and ran events including an annual staff–student conference about IGL and workshops for staff and students in academic departments, contributed to the design of new IGL initiatives, provided support for data collection in the assessment of CETL-funded IGL projects, conducted research into the student experience, contributed to national conferences, and were called on to act as advisers on student roles in educational enhancement to other institutions.

Staff Development and Networks. We organized a number of formal networks and special interest groups (such as for information literacy in IGL and for IGL scholarship) and a wide variety of IGL-related events including staff development workshops that provided experiential engagement with IGL. We placed special emphasis on fostering informal and social networking among faculty and other staff involved in any aspect of instruction and support for IGL and provided resources to support networking connections beyond the institution. Dissemination-of-practice strategies included Web-based case studies, briefing papers, and an internal newsletter with an informal, people-focused flavor and strong student visibility. We used Web 2.0 tools (including photo- and slide-sharing, blogs, a wiki, Second Life) to engage interest and disseminate information internally and externally.

Pedagogical Alignment of Physical Learning and Teaching Space. We were fortunate in having the resources to create a number of flexible, technology-rich classroom environments referred to as "inquiry collaboratories" specifically to support IGL, through refurbishment of existing space and new space within the university's Information Commons building, which also housed the CETL. The support we provided for new users among the faculty blended technical and instructional design guidance. We learned from feedback that these new spaces provided a stimulus for trying out new instructional approaches and helped to foster closer research-based partnerships both between students and between faculty and students.

Assessment, Research, and Scholarship. The blended identity of the CETL as at once a research, academic, and service center and the varied roles of its staff (including faculty interns on fellowships) was an important source of credibility with the faculty. The CETL supported and conducted scholarship of teaching and learning and research for IGL, including institutional research into staff and students' perspectives on the relationship between research and teaching.

Future Directions

Now that the CETL's funding period is over, what does the future hold for IGL at TUOS? The opportunity to conduct a five-year, high-profile development program contributed much to reinforcing the university's commitment to strengthened links between research, learning, and teaching. Many instructional initiatives supported by the development program have become part of the fabric of departmental and individual practice and are expected to be sustained and to evolve well into the future. The program's inquiry collaboratories have had direct impact on the design of other new learning and teaching spaces in the university, and this trend too is expected to continue. A new, institution-wide Student Ambassadors for Learning and Teaching initiative has been launched (www.shef.ac.uk/lets/salt) and continuing institution-level support for IGL development, in the broader context of research-led learning, has passed from the CETL to the university's central Learning and Teaching Services unit. Investment in enhancement of the student experience remains strong at TUOS, and IGL practice and related themes including information literacy are embedded into ongoing developments.

References

Bereiter, C. *Education and the Mind in the Knowledge Age.* Mahwah, N.J.: Lawrence Erlbaum Associates, 2002.

Cox, A., P. Levy, P. Stordy, and S. Webber. "Inquiry-Based Learning in the First-Year Information Management Curriculum." *ITALICS, Journal of the Information and Computer Sciences Higher Education Academy Subject Centre,* 2008, 7(1). Retrieved April 30, 2011, from www.ics.heacademy.ac.uk/italics/vol7iss1/pdf/Paper1.pdf.

Hart, D., A. G. Diercks-O'Brien, and A. Powell "Exploring Stakeholder Engagement in Impact Evaluation Planning in Educational Development Work." *Evaluation,* 2009, 15, 285–306.

Healey, M. "Linking Research and Teaching: Exploring Disciplinary Spaces and the Role of Inquiry-Based Learning." In R. Barnett (ed.), *Reshaping the University: New Relationships between Research, Scholarship and Teaching.* Buckingham, United Kingdom: Society for Research into Higher Education and Open University Press, 2005.

Healey, M., and A. Jenkins. *Developing Undergraduate Research and Inquiry.* York, United Kingdom: Higher Education Academy, 2009.

Justice, C., and others. "Inquiry in Higher Education: Reflections and Directions on Course Design and Teaching Methods." *Innovative Higher Education,* 2007, 31, 201–214.

Levy, P. "Exploring and Developing Excellence: Towards a Community of Praxis." In A. Skelton (ed.), *International Perspectives on Teaching Excellence in Higher Education.* Abingdon, Oxfordshire, United Kingdom: Routledge, 2007.

Levy, P., S. Little, and N. Whelan. "Perspectives on Staff-Student Partnership in Learning, Research and Educational Enhancement." In S. Little (ed.), *Staff-Student Partnerships in Higher Education.* London: Continuum, 2011.

Levy, P. "Embedding Inquiry and Research for Knowledge-Building into Mainstream Higher Education: A UK Perspective." *CUR Quarterly,* 2011, 32(1), 36–42.

Levy, P., and R. Petrulis. "How Do First-Year University Students Experience Inquiry and Research, and What Are the Implications for the Practice of Inquiry-Based Learning?" *Studies in Higher Education,* 2012, 37(1). doi:10.1080/03075079.2010.499166.

Levy, P., and others. *The Sheffield Companion to Inquiry-Based Learning.* Sheffield, United Kingdom: Centre for Inquiry-based Learning in the Arts and Social Sciences, University of Sheffield, 2010.

Little, S. "Oily Rag or Winged Messenger: The Role of the Developer in Multi-Professional Teams." In R. Donnelly and F. McSweeney (eds.), *Applied E-Learning and E-Teaching in Higher Education.* Hershey, Pa.: IGI Publishing, 2008.

McKinney, P., M. Jones, and S. Turkington, S. "Information Literacy through Inquiry: A Level One Psychology Module at the University of Sheffield." *Aslib Proceedings: New Information Directions*, 2011, *63* (2–3), 221–240.

Rossiter, D., R. Petrulis, and C. A. Biggs. "A Blended Approach to Problem-Based Learning in the Freshman Year." *Chemical Engineering Education*, 2010, *44*(1), 23–29.

Stafford, T. "A Fire to Be Lighted: Case Study in Enquiry-Based Learning." *Practice and Evidence of Scholarship of Teaching and Learning in Higher Education*, 2008, *3*(1), 20–42.

van Oostrum, D., R. Steadman-Jones, and Z. Carson. "Taking the Imaginative Leap: Creative Writing and Inquiry-Based Learning." *Pedagogy*, 2007, *7*(3), 556–566.

Verbaan, E. "The Multicultural Society in the Netherlands: Technology-Supported Inquiry-Based Learning in an Institutional Context." *Teaching in Higher Education*, 2008, *13*, 437–447.

Webber, S. "Investigating Models of Student Inquiry in Second Life as Part of a Blended Approach." *International Journal of Personal and Virtual Learning Environments*, 2010, *1*(3), 55–70.

Additional Resources

The CETL developed a number of resources to support instructional design for IGL, including a booklet titled *The Sheffield Companion to Inquiry-based Learning* (Levy and others, 2010), which includes an Inquiry-based Learning Planner. The booklet can be accessed at www.shef.ac.uk/ibl/resources/sheffieldcompanion. This Web site also provides access to images of the inquiry collaboratories at TUOS and a range of other IGL resources and sources of information about the CILASS program, including the final evaluation report on its activities to the Higher Education Funding Council for England.

PHILIPPA LEVY was academic director of the Centre for Inquiry-based Learning in the Arts and Social Sciences at The University of Sheffield (TUOS) between 2005 and 2010. She is currently head of the Information School at TUOS.

NEW DIRECTIONS FOR TEACHING AND LEARNING • DOI: 10.1002/tl

3

This chapter presents a case study of how inquiry-guided learning has been developed and embedded within a small university in the United Kingdom. It highlights the different theoretical and conceptual frameworks that contributed to our evolving understanding of inquiry-guided learning and the importance of recognizing and working with disciplinary differences.

Developing and Embedding Inquiry-Guided Learning Across an Institution

Martin Jenkins, Mick Healey

The University of Gloucestershire, located in the southwest of the United Kingdom, is a small university with approximately 7,500 full-time students and 400 teaching staff. It has three faculties, all with a professional or applied focus: Media, Art, and Technology; Business, Education, and Professional Studies; and Applied Sciences.

Both the University Strategic Plan and the Teaching, Learning, and Assessment Strategic Framework (TLASF) (University of Gloucestershire, 2007) recognize inquiry-guided learning (IGL), using the broader term active learning. The award of national Centre for Excellence in Teaching and Learning (CETL) status, leading to the creation of the Centre for Active Learning (CeAL), influenced the formal adoption of IGL. The CETL program was a major investment initiative in teaching and learning in English universities. Through a competitive process, successful projects received funding of up to £5 million over a five-year period. As a result, the University of Gloucestershire was able to develop and embed the use of IGL approaches within the institution.

Inquiry-Guided Learning and the Curriculum

The first priority of the University Strategic Plan (2009–12) is "Achieving Inspirational Learning." It states that the university will "continue to develop our innovation in teaching and learning founded on an enquiry-based approach and take advantage of the opportunities provided by

NEW DIRECTIONS FOR TEACHING AND LEARNING, no. 129, Spring 2012 © Wiley Periodicals, Inc.
Published online in Wiley Online Library (wileyonlinelibrary.com) • DOI: 10.1002/tl.20004

e-learning to invest in new learning technologies" (University of Gloucestershire, 2009, p. 4).

As a clear statement of intent for the institution, the priority reinforces the focus on IGL that was already present in the university. In June 2007 active engagement was included in the university's TLASF after an inclusive process involving staff and students from across the institution (Healey, Mason O'Connor, and Broadfoot, 2010). The university identified five principles for the new strategy: active engagement; learner empowerment; learning communities; learning for sustainable development; and learning for equality, diversity, and intercultural understanding. With regard to active engagement the TLASF states:

> In conjunction with their development of subject knowledge, students will be supported, through appropriate teaching and learning approaches, to develop the skills required for lifelong learning.

> A principal means for achieving this is through the promotion of active engagement in learning. Active engagement may be characterised in numerous ways including "active learning," "problem based learning," "inquiry based learning," "experiential learning," "research based learning," and "reflective learning."

> All are imbued with strong elements of scholarship, discovery and creativity. Active engagement may be promoted in ways appropriate to individual disciplines and learning styles. (University of Gloucestershire, 2007)

The Rationale and Theory Behind Inquiry-Guided Learning

Two theoretical models, Kolb's Experiential Learning Cycle (1984) and Performances for Understanding (Blythe and Associates, 1998), informed the university's initial approach to IGL as well as the concept of the teaching-research nexus. According to Kolb (1984, 38), "Learning is the process whereby knowledge is created through the transformation of experience." The theory presents a way of structuring and sequencing the curriculum at module and program levels so that students, with their diverse set of learning styles and needs, go through a range of activities that reflect the cyclical nature of learning (Fielding, 1994; Healey and Jenkins, 2000). Paraphrasing Kolb, the four stages of learning are experience, reflect, generalize, and test (Cowan, 2006).

To Kolb's approach we added the "teaching for understanding" perspective, which attends to the *kinds* of experiences we design for our students (Healey, Roberts, and Jenkins, 2005). It insists that simply "having" knowledge is insufficient because learners need to go through "performances of understanding" fully to comprehend their subject. Although developed with children in mind, the coupling of knowing and doing

Figure 3.1. The CeAL Approach to Active Learning

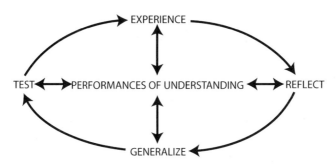

Source: Healey, Roberts, and Jenkins, 2005.

translates readily to the university context. The CeAL model of active learning as IGL appears in Figure 3.1.

The model underscores the importance of incorporating a variety of learning modes in the planning and implementation of instruction and, in conjunction with Kolb's Learning Style Inventory, assists students in understanding their individual learning style. The model also facilitates different disciplinary interpretations of active learning.

Finally, from the very beginning CeAL's approach to IGL emphasized the importance of students learning through engagement in inquiry and research (Healey and Jenkins, 2009). At the same time we recognize that there are a range of ways of linking research and teaching and that the appropriate balance between them will vary by year and discipline as well as by individual teaching styles (Healey, 2005). Levy's adaptation (2009) of Healey's model (2005) captures the range of ways of linking research and teaching along two dimensions: building new knowledge or exploring existing knowledge and between instructor-framed inquiry and student-framed inquiry (see Figure 3.2).

A Developing Understanding of Inquiry-Guided Learning

Over time other ideas and practices enriched the university's understanding of IGL as different disciplines experimented with it. An analysis of individual case studies of module and program revision using IGL across a range of disciplines by the CeAL program revealed common elements in both the implementation of IGL and the rationale for its use (Centre for Active Learning, 2010). Based on this analysis, IGL at the university shares the following key elements: collaborative learning, authentic learning experiences, reflection, skill development, and clearly identified and structured student support. The most common reasons for using IGL include learner

Figure 3.2. Model of Inquiry-Guided Learning

EXPLORING AND ACQUIRING EXISTING DISCIPLINARY KNOWLEDGE

Information-active	**Information-responsive**
Students explore the knowledge base of the discipline by pursuing questions, problems, scenarios, or lines of inquiry they themselves have formulated ("What is the existing answer to my question?")	Students explore the knowledge base of the discipline in response to questions, problems, scenarios, or lines of inquiry formulated by tutors ("What is the existing answer to this question?")
Discovery-active	**Discovery-responsive**
Students pursue new questions, problems, scenarios, or lines of inquiry they themselves have formulated, drawing on the knowledge base of the discipline ("How can I answer my question or approach this question in my new way?")	Students pursue new questions, problems, scenarios, or lines of inquiry, as formulated by tutors or others, drawing on the knowledge base of the discipline ("How can I answer this new question or approach this question in this new way?")

PARTICIPATING IN BUILDING DISCIPLINARY KNOWLEDGE

Source: Levy, 2009.

empowerment, collaborative learning, skill development and employability, encouragement of reflection, and student motivation.

Table 3.1 summarizes three key practices embedded throughout the curriculum at the university and their theoretical and practical rationales.

Embedding Inquiry-Guided Learning

Achieving significant institution-wide adoption requires flexibility in approach. Some initiatives were serendipitous (for example, digital storytelling), opportunities that arose as unplanned outcomes from other projects, taking advantage of the developments in our thinking during the program. For others CeAL took a strong advocacy position, identifying key projects in the successful implementation of IGL such as the active learning

Table 3.1. Key Practices in Inquiry-Guided Learning at the University of Gloucestershire

Practice	Description	Theory	Rationale	Researchers
Collaborative learning	Peer group, whole group, work-based learning, learning communities	Sociocultural theories	Student empowerment, reflection as social process, linkages with real-world environment	Bradbury, Frost, Kilminster, and Zukas, 2010; Wenger, 1998
Authentic learning	Fieldwork, work-based learning, real-world learning, links with community and professions	Supercomplexity	Student employability	Barnett, 2000
Reflective practice	Support for student learning, digital storytelling	Experiential learning cycle; reflection in action	Students as critical thinkers in a complex world	Dewey, 1938; Kolb, 1984; McDrury and Alterio, 2003; Moon, 1999; Schön, 1983

induction. CeAL also worked to embed support within existing processes and supported existing local pedagogic developments by providing pedagogic expertise and support for evaluation. The latter approaches have the benefit of building on existing activity and so minimize the perception that initiatives are placing additional demands on staff time.

The Active Learning Induction. The transition into higher education from secondary school is a key moment, presenting both personal and academic challenges to new students. CeAL had identified induction as an important opportunity to introduce students to IGL approaches. As part of a weeklong program integrated within the orientation week, students engaged in discipline-specific inquiry activities. By the end of the week, they completed a cycle of activity, producing a piece of work and receiving feedback from staff. Group work was central to these activities, which provided opportunities for socialization at the same time. The model for the induction week appears in Figure 3.3.

The use of a discipline-based activity was important in providing immediate immersion for the students. Example activities included conducting interviews to assess the impact of the Gloucestershire floods of 2007 on local people (sociology and human geography); conducting fieldwork to investigate the potential impact of flooding a local river valley (environmental science and physical geography); and creating and analyzing poems and plays about trees (English).

Figure 3.3. Model for Active Learning Induction Week

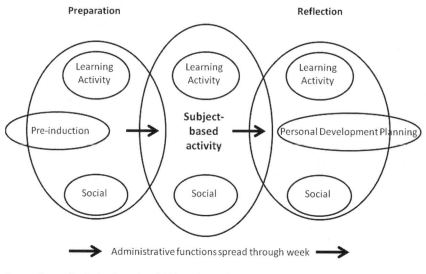

Source: Centre for Active Learning, 2009, p. 4.

In all cases students, working in groups, were required to prepare for the activity, conduct their own investigation, and present their findings to their peers. Student feedback has been consistently positive as a means of introducing students to IGL and socializing them into higher education. In addition, where adopted by whole departments or faculties, the IGL approach provides a valuable staff development opportunity, engaging both academic and learning support staff.

Induction also provided the vehicle to introduce new teaching and learning approaches such as digital storytelling, a technique that creates short movies through recorded narrative with digital media (Gravestock and Jenkins, 2009; Hartley and McWilliam, 2009). Piloted as part of induction, students, working in groups, used digital storytelling to tell the narrative of their active learning project. The value of the technique in encouraging student reflection was recognized and is now used in all three faculties. Uses include capturing student reflections on critical incidents, for example from industrial placements; as a replacement for reflective essays, thus developing digital literacies as well; as an alternative form of presentation, where it has been found to particularly benefit students who find presentations difficult or those whose first language is not English; and as a means of capturing reflection on developmental activities such as the evolution of design projects.

Broadcast Journalism "Newsweek." In the Broadcast Journalism program "Newsweek," students run their own multimedia newsroom including radio, television, and online news for an entire week (Simmons, 2009). The experience uses the learning cycle of action, reflection, and progression over a concentrated period of time in a real-world setting, thereby increasing its impact.

Designed as a final assessment, "Newsweek" is the second part of a unit of learning. The first half consists of lectures, seminars, and workshops in a room incorporating radio and television studios. In this environment students can try out various roles, such as producer, reporter, or presenter, before applying to their peer colleagues for the role they would like to adopt during "Newsweek." During the week the students produce ten 15-minute radio, television, and online news reports. Students select one program each from TV and radio plus an online story to put forward for assessment, providing a group grade worth 50 percent of the award for this unit.

The development of this assessment posed certain challenges. Colleagues were concerned about the academic rigor of the experience, and students were uncomfortable with equally shared group marks. Despite initial skepticism, however, this approach, initially used only with final-year students, is now in place at the intermediate level in Broadcast Journalism and incorporated into the documentation for new courses in journalism at the BA and MA levels.

Business Program Development. Faculty in Business Management (BM) initiated a major review of their program, identifying a need to provide an authentic and more integrated program that embraced the principles of active engagement.

CeAL provided educational support during the program development process including delivery of staff development events, consultation with individual staff, and pedagogic planning tools. CeAL also provided additional resources such as business simulation programs and extended consultation with a CeAL visiting fellow (Jones, 2008).

To evaluate the impact of the new program on student learning, a survey was conducted across all three levels of BM: level I of the new BM and levels II and III of the old course. The questions targeted the degree of perceived academic challenge and the nature of the learning experience. The sample of responses in Table 3.2 indicates that students in the new BM program were more engaged, showing more emphasis on synthesis and organization and less on knowledge transmission, than did students on levels II and III of the old course. The students in the new BM course also considered themselves more active participants in the learning process and involved in discovery processes.

Other Aspects of the Implementation

The institutional adoption of IGL at the University of Gloucestershire is representative of a bottom-up approach through individual project

Table 3.2. Student Survey Results from Business Management Program at the University of Gloucestershire

Academic achievement During the current academic year, how much has your coursework emphasized the following academic activities? [10 = very much, 0 = very little]	Level 1 Mean N = 58 (new program)	Level 2 Mean N = 17 (old program)	Level 3 Mean N = 29 (old program)
Memorizing facts, ideas, methods, or formulae from your lectures, seminars, or self-study so they can be repeated or used in more or less the same form	5.53	5.76	6.52
Analyzing the basic elements of an idea, experience, or theory, such as examining a particular case or situation in-depth and considering its components	6.72	6.94	6.69
Synthesizing and organizing ideas, information, or experiences into new, more complex interpretations or relationships	6.55	6.41	5.91
Making judgments about the value of information, arguments, or methods, such as examining how others gathered and interpreted data and assessing the soundness of their conclusions	6.38	6.35	5.86
Applying theories or concepts to practical problems or in new situations	6.90	6.53	6.38
How would you characterize the balance of the way you have been taught this year across your whole program? [on a 0–10 scale]			
Students as active participants, i.e., student focused [=10] vs. students as passive audience, i.e. teacher focused [=0]	6.43	6.35	5.57
Emphasis on learning how knowledge is constructed and engaging in the research/discovery process [=10] vs. emphasis on learning about the results of current research and knowledge [=0]	6.14	5.94	5.41
Activities			
This year, about how often have you done each of the following? [10 = very much, 0 = very little]			
Worked with other students on projects during class	9.07	6.53	7.14
Worked with other students outside of class in groups formally established to work on set activities or assignments	7.71	6.71	5.83
To what extent has your experience at university this year contributed to your skills and personal development in the following areas? [10 = very much, 0 = very little]			
Thinking critically	6.79	6.71	6.93

developments supported by the CeAL program and of a top-down initiative through the University Strategic Plan and TLASF. However, in some cases there was a disjunction between bottom-up and top-down approaches that became a barrier to innovation. Possible reasons for the disjuncture include pressures on staff time in delivering programs and systems and structural processes that are resistant to change and new ideas. In addition, some departmental managers took these projects as an opportunity to procure additional resources without full commitment to the outcomes; support at this level is important for the success of programs. In all cases it was critical that faculty took ownership of the process (Healey, Mason O'Connor, and Broadfoot, 2010).

Conclusions

Although the university has achieved considerable success in the development and embedding of IGL across the institution, the process has not always been straightforward. The need to allow flexibility in the interpretation of IGL was an important lesson learned during the CeAL program. The typology of active learning (Centre for Active Learning, 2010) identified common elements within the university but with variations among the disciplines. In addition, research undertaken during the CeAL program indicates that how academic staff interpret IGL relates to their conceptions of teaching and learning, which can have disciplinary influences. The difference in interpretation of IGL relates to instructors' own focus of attention: themselves and their teaching or students and their learning (Romer, 2009; Wright, 2010).

Even with significant investment through the government-supported CETL program, successful implementation came down to the successful integration of institutional strategy and discipline-based initiatives. In addition, individual staff members need respect and the space to develop their own understandings of IGL, ideally through their own inquiry into new teaching and learning approaches.

References

Barnett, R. *Realizing the University in an Age of Supercomplexity.* Buckingham, United Kingdom: Society for Research into Higher Education/Open University Press, 2000.

Blythe, T., and Associates. *The Teaching for Understanding Guide.* San Francisco: Jossey-Bass, 1998.

Bradbury, H., N. Frost, S. Kilminster, and M. Zukas. *Beyond Reflective Practice: New Approaches to Professional Lifelong Learning.* Abingdon, United Kingdom: Routledge, 2010.

Centre for Active Learning. *The introduction of an active learning induction.* Cheltenham, United Kingdom: CeAL, University of Gloucestershire, 2009. Retrieved December 7, 2011, from http://insight.glos.ac.uk/tli/resources/toolkit/wal/sustainable/Pages/ActiveLearningInduction.aspx.

Centre for Active Learning. *Active Learning Typology.* Cheltenham, United Kingdom: CeAL, University of Gloucestershire, 2010. Retrieved February 7, 2011, from http://insight.glos.ac.uk/tli/resources/toolkit/wal/Pages/ActiveLearningTypology.aspx.

Cowan, J. *On Becoming an Innovative University Teacher: Reflection in Action.* 2nd ed. Maidenhead, United Kingdom: Open University, 2006.

Dewey, J. *Experience and Education.* New York: Collier Books, 1938.

Fielding, M. "Valuing Difference in Teachers and Learners: Building on Kolb's Learning Styles to Develop a Language of Teaching and Learning." *Curriculum Journal,* 1994, 5(3), 393–417.

Gravestock, P., and M. Jenkins. "Digital Storytelling and Its Pedagogical Impact." In T. Mayes and others (eds.), *Transforming Higher Education through Technology-enhanced Learning.* York, United Kingdom: Higher Education Academy, 2009.

Hartley, J., and K. McWilliam, eds. *Story Circle: Digital Storytelling around the World.* Chichester, United Kingdom: Wiley-Blackwell, 2009.

Healey, M. "Linking Research and Teaching Exploring Disciplinary Spaces and the Role of Inquiry-based Learning." In R. Barnett (ed.), *Reshaping the University: New Relationships between Research, Scholarship and Teaching.* Maidenhead, United Kingdom: McGraw-Hill/Open University Press, 2005.

Healey, M., and A. Jenkins. "Learning Cycles and Learning Styles: The Application of Kolb's Experiential Learning Model in Higher Education." *Journal of Geography,* 2000, 99, 185–195.

Healey, M., and A. Jenkins. *Developing Undergraduate Research and Inquiry.* York, United Kingdom: Higher Education Academy, 2009. Retrieved April 3, 2011, from http://www.heacademy.ac.uk/assets/York/documents/resources/publications/DevelopingUndergraduate_Final.pdf.

Healey, M., K. Mason O'Connor, and P. Broadfoot. "Reflecting on Engaging Students in the Process and Product of Strategy Development for Learning, Teaching and Assessment: An Institutional Example." *International Journal for Academic Development,* 2010, 15(1), 19–32.

Healey, M., C. Roberts, and M. Jenkins. "Researching and Evaluating Active and Inquiry-based Learning in Geography in Higher Education." Paper presented at Researching and Evaluating Research-based Learning in CETLs Symposium, C-SAP, University of Birmingham, Birmingham, United Kingdom, December 15, 2005.

Jones, A. *Report on the Introduction of the New BM in the Business School, University of Gloucestershire.* CeAL Visiting Fellowship Report, 2008. Retrieved February 7, 2011, from http://insight.glos.ac.uk/tli/resources/toolkit/eal/Pages/VisitingFellows.aspx.

Kolb, D. A. *Experiential Learning: Experience as a Source of Learning and Development.* New York: Prentice Hall, 1984.

Levy, P. *Inquiry-based Learning: A Conceptual Framework (Version 4).* Sheffield,United Kingdom: Centre for Inquiry-based Learning in the Arts and Social Sciences, University of Sheffield, 2009. Retrieved November 15, 2011, from http://www.shef.ac.uk/content/1/c6/09/37/83/CILASS%20IBL%20Framework%20(Version%204).doc.

McDrury, J., and M. G. Alterio. *Learning through Storytelling in Higher Education Using Reflection and Experience to Improve Learning.* London: Kogan Page, 2003.

Moon, J. A. *Reflection in Learning and Professional Development: Theory and Practice.* Abingdon, United Kingdom: Routledge Falmer, 1999.

Romer, W. *Perceptions of Active Learning Report.* Centre for Active Learning (CeAL) Project 07–05, 2009. Retrieved February 7, 2011, from http://insight.glos.ac.uk/tli/resources/toolkit/wal/perceptions/Pages/default.aspx.

Schön, D. *The Reflective Practitioner: How Professionals Think in Action.* New York: Basic Books, 1983.

Simmons, C. *Broadcast Journalism Newsweek*. Centre for Active Learning (CeAL) Project 07–15, 2009. Retrieved February 7, 2011, from http://insight.glos.ac.uk/tli/resources /toolkit/wal/sustainable/Pages/Newsweek.aspx.

University of Gloucestershire. *Teaching, Learning and Assessment Strategic Framework, University of Gloucestershire*, 2007.

University of Gloucestershire. *Strategic Plan 2009–12: Sustaining, Pioneering, Transforming*, 2009. Cheltenham, United Kingdom: University of Gloucestershire. Retrieved April 3, 2011, from http://resources.glos.ac.uk/publications/strategicplan /index.cfm.

Wenger, E. *Communities of Practice: Learning, Meaning and Identity*. Cambridge, United Kingdom: Cambridge University Press, 1998.

Wright, P. *A Cross Institutional View of Active Learning*. Centre for Active Learning (CeAL) Project 07–27, 2010. Retrieved February 7, 2011, from http://insight.glos .ac.uk/tli/activities/activelearning/projects/Pages/6.aspx.

MARTIN JENKINS is manager of the Centre for Educational Development, Christchurch Polytechnic Institute of Technology, New Zealand. He was formerly academic manager, Centre for Active Learning, University of Gloucestershire, United Kingdom.

MICK HEALEY is a higher education consultant and researcher and emeritus professor at the University of Gloucestershire, United Kingdom.

4

This chapter describes a range of inquiry-guided learning methods from an "appetizer" to an "entrée" approach at two universities in New Zealand. Suggestions are provided for instructors and course designers considering using an inquiry approach.

Inquiry-Guided Learning in New Zealand: From an Appetizer to an Entrée

Billy O'Steen, Rachel Spronken-Smith

The Menu of Tertiary Education in New Zealand

New Zealand is unique in the global tertiary education environment because there is a legislative requirement that teaching and research are closely interdependent and that most teaching in universities and all degree-granting institutions should be done by people who are active in advancing knowledge (New Zealand Government, 1989). Moreover, the Tertiary Education Strategy calls for "a research culture within which undergraduates learn to take a research-based approach to their lifelong educational development" (New Zealand Ministry of Education, 2002, 60). Thus there is a strong imperative for research and inquiry to be part of the undergraduate curriculum.

In 2006 the authors were part of a research team that gained a substantial external grant from the government to document and analyze the use of inquiry-guided learning (IGL) in undergraduate education in New Zealand (see Spronken-Smith and others, 2008). This chapter draws on that research by first providing some background on the research project and highlighting some key findings and then considering different approaches to including IGL in an undergraduate curriculum. In the first case—the appetizer, we discuss how inquiry can be included in a large first-year sociology class, and in the second case—the entrée—we examine how inquiry is embedded throughout an ecology degree program. The intent is

New Directions for Teaching and Learning, no. 129, Spring 2012 © Wiley Periodicals, Inc.
Published online in Wiley Online Library (wileyonlinelibrary.com) • DOI: 10.1002/tl.20005

to present theoretical concepts from the research and to offer practical advice for faculty seeking to include inquiry within an undergraduate curriculum.

The Research Ingredients

The research project involved a collaborative team across four institutions: University of Canterbury (Billy Osteen), University of Otago (Rachel Spronken-Smith and Rebecca Walker), Victoria University of Wellington (Tom Angelo, now at La Trobe University, Melbourne), and the Christchurch Polytechnic Institute of Technology (Julie Batchelor and Helen Matthews). In each institution a purposive sample of three to four cases of IGL was collected across a range of levels and disciplines (Table 4.1). The research aimed to provide case studies of IGL and to undertake a meta-analysis of the cases to explore the key questions of what factors are conducive or prohibitive to using IGL in undergraduate curricula in New Zealand.

Table 4.1. Overview of the Fourteen Cases of IGL Selected for Research

University of Otago	University of Canterbury	Victoria University of Wellington	Christchurch Polytechnic Institute of Technology
Stage 2 guided, information-oriented inquiry course: Political Communication	Stage 1 mixed mode, mainly information-oriented inquiry course: Sociology	Stage 1 guided information-oriented inquiry course: History	Level 4 guided, information-oriented inquiry course: Fashion Technology & Design
Stage 3 structured, information-oriented inquiry module*: Endocrinology	Stage 1 guided, discovery-oriented inquiry course: Engineering	Stage 1 structured, information-oriented inquiry course: Psychology	Stage 2 open, information and discovery-oriented inquiry course: Outdoor Education
Stage 3 open, discovery-oriented inquiry course: Ecology Field Course	Stage 3 open, discovery-oriented course: Communication Disorders	Stage 2 open, discovery-oriented inquiry course: Architecture	Stage 2 open, discovery-oriented inquiry course: Radio Production and Performance
Ecology Degree Program		Stage 3 open, discovery-oriented inquiry course: International Business	

*A module runs for about eight weeks and has four contact hours a week.

NEW DIRECTIONS FOR TEACHING AND LEARNING • DOI: 10.1002/tl

Tasters from the Research

One of the key outcomes of our research was developing a theoretical and grounded framework for inquiry approaches (Spronken-Smith and Walker, 2010). Given that inquiry had often been used as an umbrella term to encompass a range of approaches, we attempted to tease out just what these approaches were in a more systematic way. The result was a framework for inquiry with three criteria: scale, mode, and framing. Regarding scale, it is important to describe whether the inquiry activities are occurring in a class, in a course, or as a design principle for a whole course or degree. For mode, we drew on the work of Staver and Bay (1987) to recognize three categories:

- *Structured inquiry*—instructors provide an issue or problem and an outline for addressing it.
- *Guided inquiry*—instructors provide questions to stimulate inquiry but students are self-directed in terms of exploring these questions.
- *Open inquiry*—students formulate the questions themselves as well as going through the full inquiry cycle: engage with a topic, develop a question, identify what needs to be known, collect and analyze data, synthesize findings, communicate results, and evaluate the research (Justice and others, 2007).

For framing, we used Levy's (2009) research that identified:

- *Information-oriented inquiry*—students conduct research that seeks already existing answers with the purpose of acquiring a given body of knowledge (for example, many lower-level science labs).
- *Discovery-oriented inquiry*—students understand and conduct research in terms of personal questioning, exploration, and discovery in relation to new questions or lines of investigation (for example, many upper-level, master's, or doctoral courses).

Our definition is thus akin to Beckman and Hensel's (2009) definition for undergraduate research, with an important caveat: in IGL the approach should be student centered, which is not always the case for undergraduate research (Spronken-Smith, 2010).

The culmination of the meta-analysis was a conceptual model (Figure 4.1) showing the relationship between different modes and framing of inquiry and either the strength of the research-teaching nexus or enhanced learning outcomes. The greatest potential for a strong research-teaching nexus occurs with open, discovery-oriented inquiry. Similarly, open, discovery-oriented inquiry provides the greatest opportunity for enhanced learning outcomes. However, inquiry can encompass a range of tasks in both information and discovery-oriented frames and in a variety of modes to progressively develop research and inquiry skills. The model is deliberately constructed in a stepped, podium fashion to illustrate the scaffolding

Figure 4.1. Conceptual Model of the Relation between the Focus of Learning and the Level of Independence for Different Modes and Framing of Inquiry

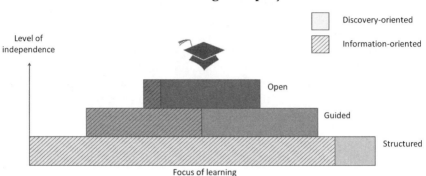

As the level of shading increases, there is greater potential for a stronger research-teaching nexus (Spronken-Smith and Walker, 2010) and students perceive learning outcomes to be enhanced (Spronken-Smith and others, forthcoming). Ideally students should experience open inquiry before graduation.

metaphor (with more guidance provided at the base) and the desire that graduates should attain the highest level before graduation (Spronken-Smith and Walker, 2010). However, although one model of embedding inquiry within a degree is to have structured inquiry for first-year students, guided for second-year students, and open for third-year students, another approach is to start with open inquiry at first year so that students are introduced early to the vagaries of research (see Healey and Jenkins, 2009; Justice, Rice, and Warry, 2009; Wood and Levy, 2009).

In the following cases, we illustrate how IGL can be used in a large, first-year sociology class through mixed mode, mainly information-oriented IGL. In the second case we describe how IGL has been embedded in an ecology degree program, progressively developing research and inquiry skills.

The Appetizer: Sociology 111 at the University of Canterbury

Sociology 111: Exploring Society is an introductory course that has no prerequisites but is required for a sociology major within the Bachelor of Arts. Its design and delivery have been redesigned by Brigid Thompson, a graduate of the program, who became the course coordinator. The main goal of the course is students' development of thinking like sociologists in the context of contemporary sociological topics such as crime, death and dying, food, sexuality, and sports. To carry the food metaphor further, she desired for students to become their own chefs and not merely remain as consumers of others' fare.

NEW DIRECTIONS FOR TEACHING AND LEARNING • DOI: 10.1002/tl

The design and delivery of the course reflected this division of content and process. The specific topics were taught by a team of faculty members whose specific research interests made up the content of the course. They presented their topics through large lectures (200–300 students) in one session per week. The process of learning to think like a sociologist was facilitated through weekly interactive tutorials taught by Brigid with smaller groups of fifty students each. The tutorials used a guided mode of inquiry by leading students to develop personally relevant questions about the sociological topics in the lectures. Thus, in a high-enrollment course with multiple instructors and topics, IGL was the most important thread of consistency.

It is important to note that Brigid was motivated to redesign the course around IGL based on her own experiences as a student in the course. She described the previous versions of the course as also using the guest lecture approach, but without an explicitly strong thread to hold those sessions together. She believed that by using the theme of "thinking like a sociologist" through asking sociological questions, she would give both the guest lecturers and the students a focus for the course that encompassed all topics. Beyond just this course, however, she also did some informal research with her colleagues to find out what they wanted and expected students to be able to do in the second- and third-year courses. This research supported and evolved into the notion of assisting students in developing and asking questions like sociologists and preparing them for an eventual open mode of inquiry-based learning.

The Entrée: Ecology at the University of Otago

At the University of Otago, ecology is offered through a modular degree structure with students taking a mixture of required ecology courses and other required courses (such as biology, physical geography, statistics) and some optional courses. The ecology program is taught by an interdisciplinary team, with faculty from Botany, Zoology, Philosophy, Marine Science, and Higher Education. Because of the modular degree structure, teachers have control over only the five core ecology courses, and four of these use inquiry components. Following a New Zealand university audit, which focused on the links between research and teaching, and a program review, which called for more research experiences, the ecology degree was redesigned in an explicit attempt to provide undergraduates with opportunities to develop research skills. The result is a core curriculum that progressively develops inquiry and research skills. Similar to the sociology case, the program director, Kath Dickinson, had an overall aim to educate students to think like ecologists. Table 4.2 shows four core courses and the nature of the inquiry activities in the new curriculum (for full details, see Spronken-Smith and others, 2011).

Table 4.2. Core Ecology Courses and Type of Inquiry Activities

Course	Nature of inquiry component	Assessment of inquiry component(s)
ECOL111: Ecology and Conservation of Diversity	Structured inquiry: Field and laboratory project on invertebrate biodiversity	Biodiversity report (20%)
ECOL211: Ecology of Communities and Ecosystems	Guided inquiry: Research project on an ecosystem	Group scientific poster (10%), group research proposal (10%), contribution to group work (5%)
ECOL212: Ecological Applications	Guided inquiry: Reviewing and discussing approaches to key ecological questions	Short article (10%), major essay (25%)
ECOL313: Ecology Field Course	Open inquiry: Generation and execution of research project	Participation in field course (5%), proposal presentation (5%), project preparation and fieldwork (10%), project presentation (20%), project report (50%)

Source: Smith and others, 2011b.

ECOL 111: Ecology and Conservation of Diversity, with about 140–160 students, was taught in a traditional format over a single semester with three lectures a week and one laboratory most weeks. The aim of the course was to teach fundamental ecological knowledge and approaches to understand patterns of biodiversity and manage threatened species for conservation. The structured inquiry element was a biodiversity project taught through five laboratories. In this project students worked in pairs, undertaking a pilot study in the field to learn both technical skills of doing ecological fieldwork and the value of observation and thought. The pilot study involved comparing two contrasting plant diversity levels and considering what factors were influencing this diversity. A hypothesis was then generated concerning factors that influence the abundance of leaf litter invertebrates. Students then had to create and implement a sampling design to test the hypothesis, collecting and analyzing data. Finally they had to write about the results in a scientific style, with assistance provided on analysis and writing by teaching assistants (Spronken-Smith and others, 2011).

ECOL 211: Ecology of Communities and Ecosystems, with about 75 students, was also taught in a traditional format with two lectures a week and ten laboratories in a semester. Within the laboratory sessions, a guided inquiry element was introduced in which tutors facilitated group work exploring selected ecosystems. The first inquiry task was guided and information oriented; students researched the relations between three given ecosystem components and had to produce a poster presenting their results (worth 10 percent of the final grade). Then tutors introduced a perturbation (disturbance) to the ecosystem and the groups had to generate an original question that resulted from this perturbation. Subsequently, groups had to produce a research proposal (open, discovery-oriented inquiry) using the standard university template for internal research grants. This proposal was peer reviewed and groups had to incorporate feedback in their final submission (Spronken-Smith and others, 2011).

ECOL 212: Ecological Applications, with about 60–70 students, sought to develop students' understanding of the steps involved in approaching ecology research. Although it had a traditional format with two lectures a week and a series of laboratory session, the course was focused on discussion and exploration, rather than covering set content. The teachers critiqued their own research and explored various methodological approaches, as well as discussing the social side of science, including the roles of professional societies, conferences, and jobs. There were two guided inquiry components: a major essay in which students reviewed and critiqued a major theoretical question and a short article derived from the essay, in which students summarized core arguments for a nonspecialist audience (Spronken-Smith and others, 2011).

ECOL 313: Ecology Field Course, a capstone course for about 35 students, aimed to develop field research skills as well as foster an appreciation for the realities of field research. The course used open, discovery-oriented inquiry, as students undertook the full inquiry cycle by generating a research question and then designing fieldwork to address the question, collecting and analyzing data, and writing a report in the style of a scientific paper. In addition to a written report, students had to give oral presentations for both the proposal and the findings (Spronken-Smith and others, 2011).

Lessons and Implications for Inquiry Chefs

In the case of SOCI 111, the process of curriculum change with IGL was an individual initiative undertaken by the course coordinator. The use of IGL was entirely dependent on her efforts to bring together a wide-ranging introductory buffet course that was team taught by different sociology lecturers who each focused on their specific research interests. It is unclear whether IGL will survive in this course without the presence and continued efforts of Brigid. Thus, its lasting impact as a sustained pedagogy within that major may be as ephemeral as a wonderful, yet vaguely remembered appetizer before a more standard main course.

In contrast, with the ecology degree, the process of changing the curriculum to an inquiry approach was not an individual one, but rather required considerable collaborative planning and time to implement (Spronken-Smith and others, 2011). The key factors in bringing about this change are illustrated in Figure 4.2. External drivers included the academic audit and program review, both of which gave a strong mandate for an

Figure 4.2. Conceptual Model of the Process of Curriculum Change in the University of Otago Case Study

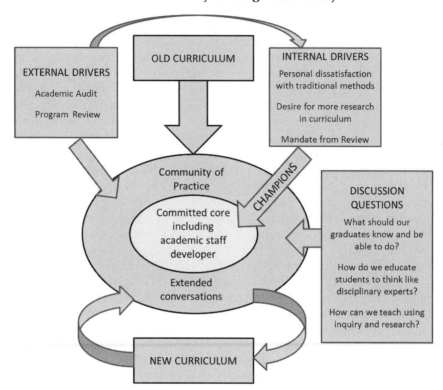

Source: Spronken-Smith and others, 2011.

inquiry approach throughout the degree. The internal drivers included a program director who championed the change and the formation of a community of practice (CoP) (Lave and Wenger, 2009) among academics committed to the change. An academic staff developer with a background in ecology and who was an activist for inquiry facilitated the regular meetings of the CoP. Conversations focused on the attributes of an ideal ecology graduate, how to educate students to think like disciplinary experts, and how to teach using inquiry and research. Moreover, the holistic consideration of the degree allowed the development of a coherent program, progressively building research skills and capabilities (Spronken-Smith and others, 2011).

The comfort level of the instructor and her or his perceived effectiveness using IGL are the main considerations of deciding between the appetizer approach of using a structured mode of IGL in an introductory course or the entrée approach of using all modes of IGL in a deliberately designed program. A comparison of student responses to an IGL survey for these two

**Figure 4.3. Comparison of Student Perceptions of the Type
of Learning Encouraged in SOCI 111 and ECOL 313**

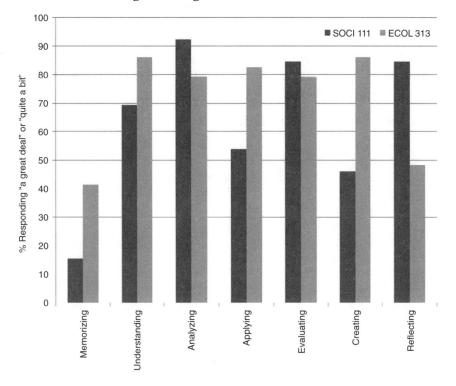

courses shows that even in small bites, students perceive higher-order learning outcomes based on Bloom's taxonomy (Figure 4.3). In fact, first-year students in SOCI 111 rated analyzing, evaluating, and reflecting more highly than did the third-year students in the ecology course. However, when considering their experience of inquiry across the whole degree, ecology students benefited significantly from the entrée approach. Representative student comments included:

> The way the program is structured helped me to develop the necessary research skills for each level and therefore prepare me for the next levels at the same time.

> My knowledge has gone from inquiry into many ecological questions to thinking that I can answer a question, if it arises, without the help of others.

The appetizer approach at Canterbury would be readily adaptable for any discipline and size of course and still achieve important outcomes with regard to students' ability to ask questions, pursue personally motivated research, and gain comfort in seeing that scholarly inquiry is often a complex endeavor with little certainty. The entrée approach at Otago is still adaptable for any discipline but requires a more significant investment of belief, effort, and planning across more faculty members. Lone chefs or solitary advocates of an IGL approach can go only so far, whereas a whole team's use of it across a major can build on all of the students' experiences and develop their undergraduate research skills.

Students' Changing Expectations

We believe that the context of K-12 education in New Zealand, which changed rather dramatically in 2010, will lead to students expecting and perhaps demanding that universities adopt the entrée approach used by the Otago ecology program. Instead of the previous focus on students' digestion of a lengthy list of discipline-based content, all schools in New Zealand are now required to develop and implement school-specific curricula based on five key competencies: thinking; using language, symbols, and text; managing self; relating to others; and participating and contributing. The role of IGL is both explicit in the new *New Zealand Curriculum* document (New Zealand Ministry of Education, 2007) (with the term *inquiry* appearing eighteen times in its forty-nine pages) and in the advice of the Ministry of Education to teachers concerning what their students should be doing:

- Take an active role in decisions about the content, process, and assessment of learning
- Take an active role in learning
- Wait less and learn more
- Be interested in their learning
- Feel empowered to make suggestions
- Ask questions of themselves, the teacher, and others (New Zealand Ministry of Education, 2011)

The implications for this shift in K-12 education will be significant for universities in that entering students may no longer be as content as they have been to passively sit in vast lecture theaters and listen to presentations delivered only from a structured, information-oriented approach. Will New Zealand universities respond proactively to this changing situation in facilitating the development of chefs instead of consumers?

References

Beckman, M., and N. Hensel. "Making Explicit the Implicit: Defining Undergraduate Research." *CUR Quarterly*, 2009, 29(4), 40–44.

Healey, M., and A. Jenkins *Developing Undergraduate Research and Inquiry*. Research Report to the Higher Education Academy. York, United Kingdom: Higher Education Academy, 2009. Retrieved February 11, 2011, from http://www.heacademy.ac.uk /assets/York/documents/resources/publications/DevelopingUndergraduate_Final.pdf.

Justice, C., J. Rice, and W. Warry. "Academic Skill Development—Inquiry Seminars Can Make a Difference: Evidence from a Quasi-Experimental Study." *International Journal of Scholarship of Teaching and Learning*, 2009, *3*(1), 1–23.

Justice, C., and others. "Inquiry in Higher Education: Reflections and Directions on Course Design and Teaching Methods." *Innovative Higher Education*, 2007, *31*(4), 201–214.

Lave, J., and E. Wenger. *Situated Learning: Legitimate Peripheral Participation*. New York: Cambridge University Press, 2009.

Levy, P. *Inquiry-based Learning: A Conceptual Framework*. Sheffield, UK: Centre for Inquiry-based Learning in the Arts and Social Sciences, University of Sheffield, 2009. Retrieved March 16, 2011, from http://www.sheffield.ac.uk/content/1/c6/09/37/83/CILASS%20IBL%20Framework%20%28Version%204%29.doc.

New Zealand Government. *Education Act, 1989*. Wellington, New Zealand: Government Printer, 1989.

New Zealand Ministry of Education. *Tertiary Education Strategy 2002/07*. Wellington, New Zealand: Ministry of Education, 2002.

New Zealand Ministry of Education. *The New Zealand Curriculum*. Wellington, New Zealand: Learning Media Ltd., 2007.

New Zealand Ministry of Education. *What Could Key Competencies Look Like in Teaching?* Key Competencies Online, 2011. Retrieved March 16, 2011, from http://keycompetencies.tki.org.nz/In-teaching.

Spronken-Smith, R. A. "Undergraduate Research and Inquiry-based Learning: Is There a Difference? Insights from Research in New Zealand." *CUR Quarterly*, 2010, *30*(4), 28–35.

Spronken-Smith, R., and R. Walker. "Can Inquiry-based Learning Strengthen the Links between Teaching and Disciplinary Research?" *Studies in Higher Education*, 2010, *35*(6), 723–740.

Spronken-Smith, R. A., and others. *Inquiry-based Learning*. Prepared for the New Zealand Ministry of Education, 2008. Retrieved March 5, 2010, from http://akoaotearoa.ac.nz/projects/inquiry-based-learning.

Spronken-Smith, R., and others. "Redesigning a Curriculum for Inquiry: An Ecology Case Study." *Instructional Science*, 2011, *39*(5), 721–735.

Spronken-Smith, R., and others. "Evaluating Student Perceptions of Learning Processes and Intended Learning Outcomes under Inquiry Approaches." *Assessment and Evaluation in Higher Education*, forthcoming.

Staver, J. R., and M. Bay. "Analysis of the Project Synthesis Goal Cluster Orientation and Inquiry Emphasis of Elementary Science Textbooks." *Journal of Research in Science Teaching*, 1987, *24*, 629–643.

Wood, J., and P. Levy. "Inquiry-based Learning Pedagogies in the Arts and Social Sciences: Purposes, Conceptions and Models of Practice." In *Proceedings of Improving Student Learning (ISL)*, September 1–3, 2008, University of Durham, Durham, United Kingdom. 2009.

BILLY O'STEEN *is a senior lecturer of higher education in the College of Education at the University of Canterbury, New Zealand.*

RACHEL SPRONKEN-SMITH *is associate professor in higher education and geography and head of the Higher Education Development Centre at the University of Otago, New Zealand.*

5

Just as inquiry-guided learning requires that students begin with questions, so does successful faculty development. At Virginia Wesleyan, this faculty inquiry process became the catalyst for more comprehensive curricular reform using inquiry-guided learning.

Questions That Matter: Using Inquiry-Guided Faculty Development to Create an Inquiry-Guided Learning Curriculum

Lisa Carstens, Joyce Bernstein Howell

The term *assessment* sends shivers down academic spines. For faculty, it signals marching orders from external parties who may or may not appreciate the subtle and not always quantifiable value of faculty efforts. For administrators, it means the dual challenge of recalibrating internal measures to meet external mandates but also inspiring faculty to recognize how those external mandates can lead to genuine growth. The story of introducing inquiry-guided learning (IGL) to Virginia Wesleyan College (VWC) is a story of turning external assessment–driven beginnings into internally meaningful and comprehensive pedagogical reform. It is especially a story of drawing upon the model of IGL itself to enable faculty to work collectively toward the common goal of being more effective teachers.

Our story begins in 2005, with the anticipation of a Southern Association of Schools and Colleges regional reaccreditation visit requiring a new component: the creation of a quality enhancement plan (QEP) identifying a major, five-year educational initiative promising measurable increases in student learning. Conversations among the eighty-odd full-time faculty of this Methodist-affiliated liberal arts college of 1,400 students had come to center on freshman experience. There was general agreement that we should focus on the seemingly recalcitrant problem of helping our new freshmen transition from being passive high school learners to becoming active and self-directed college learners. Having immersed themselves in

NEW DIRECTIONS FOR TEACHING AND LEARNING, no. 129, Spring 2012 © Wiley Periodicals, Inc.
Published online in Wiley Online Library (wileyonlinelibrary.com) • DOI: 10.1002/tl.20006

51

the literature of best practices in higher education, the faculty steering committee charged with refining a proposal embraced a plan to redesign our one-credit first-year seminar in line with key recommendations of the Boyer Commission's *Reinventing Undergraduate Education* (1998). (Other key documents influencing our approach are listed under "Additional Resources.") Thus, in place of an existing course focused on social transition, the steering committee proposed a course focused on IGL.

The faculty, briefed in recent scholarship on the power of IGL, envisioned the revision of the seminar as a natural extension of VWC best practices. Indeed, the institution had always prioritized excellence in teaching, and there were many innovative practices among the faculty, albeit in silos. However, the first wave of faculty recruited to implement this new program was not as centrally engaged in the development of the plan. They heard the term *inquiry-guided learning* as jargon and a threat to their own tried-and-true approaches to teaching. It would be unfair to dismiss these suspicions as self-satisfied resistance to change. What these faculty members really contested was in fact the very thing that we wanted students to contest through IGL: that without challenge or serious independent inquiry, they should passively accept the latest claim to truth.

And so began an internal process of faculty inquiry that led not only to the initially planned implementation of a new first-year seminar but also to a deeper and broader exploration of educational practices at Virginia Wesleyan.

Inquiry-Guided Program Design

The title of Virginia Wesleyan's quality enhancement plan was "To Engage Students in Learning by Inquiry." The purpose of this plan was to improve student learning by facilitating student engagement in inquiry-based learning practices. In the design of the first-year seminar, the steering committee focused on inquiry as a route to achieving critical thinking and information literacy objectives.

In the spring semester prior to the initial implementation, twenty-eight full-time faculty members from across the disciplines signed on to teach the seminar. The spring prelaunch phase consisted of a series of six workshops designed and facilitated by the steering committee. The workshops were intended to prepare faculty to deliver what were supposed to be incontrovertibly valuable course objectives.

At the first workshop, however, several faculty civilly but swiftly rejected the assumptions that these terms had self-evident meaning or value. What was so magical about the idea of IGL? Told that research showed that the most effective learning was driven by questions whose solutions students were to seek out for themselves, faculty objected that new freshmen also needed a foundation of knowledge; sometimes lecturing was the most effective and certainly the most efficient way to provide that foundation. Besides, on what research were these claims for IGL based?

Faculty objected, in the second place, to the idea that a one-credit first semester course could successfully teach freshmen to be "critical thinkers"—even if we were to come to a shared understanding of what "critical thinking" meant. Isn't that what we do in all our classes? Don't we believe that it takes years to develop those skills? And doesn't developmental psychology teach us both that eighteen-year-old brains are not yet sufficiently developed for certain critical thinking abilities and that the development of critical thinking powers is recursive rather than a linear movement from simple to complex? Besides, even if we build in assessment exercises to measure students' skills before and after the course, do we really believe that we can isolate what will happen in this one-credit class sufficiently to declare that any measurable gains are due to this one course?

Grudgingly, the facilitators recognized that the faculty members were bringing the discussion back to a necessary beginning. Hence, rather than a series of sessions in which faculty would be trained to implement preordained objectives and pedagogies, these workshops became interactive explorations of IGL.

Not surprisingly, controversy proved energizing. We began by working toward a common understanding of IGL. It would not be enough to accept a definition out of a book. To relate to it and support it, faculty needed to articulate it for themselves. We began with the simple and flexible definition offered by Virginia S. Lee in *Teaching and Learning Through Inquiry* (2004, p. 5): IGL "refers to a range of strategies used to promote learning through students' active, and increasingly independent, investigation of questions, problems and issues, often for which there is no single answer."

Through debate and collaboration we came to focus particularly on what struck us as the most fundamental starting point for new freshmen: learning begins with asking effective questions. For the first-year seminar syllabus, we developed this definition:

> Inquiry-guided learning describes a range of activities that have in common the student's central role as someone who actively takes charge of his or her learning, raising questions, challenging pre-packaged answers, seeking out necessary information, weighing different perspectives against one another, and making real choices about what to believe and what to do. An education founded on inquiry, then, is one that emphasizes learning processes rather than a set of answers. In First-Year Seminar, we will focus particularly on how to ask questions that matter.

Defining inquiry in terms of questions reflected not only the broader faculty's consensus about how to understand the concept of IGL but also their sense of how to connect it to critical thinking.

NEW DIRECTIONS FOR TEACHING AND LEARNING • DOI: 10.1002/tl

Initially, the steering committee had articulated the critical thinking objective broadly as "Students will develop critical thinking skills." Now faculty broke the critical thinking course goal into six more specific learning objectives and shifted the information literacy goal into the freshmen composition program. By year three, faculty would refine the six learning objectives to the three that we have maintained since:

1. Students will learn to frame productive questions in response to complex issues, questions that lead to more effective critical analysis and inquiry.
2. Students will learn how different disciplinary perspectives raise different kinds of questions and will be able to relate those different kinds of questions to the frames of reference categories in Virginia Wesleyan's general studies as well as to the purpose of a liberal arts education.
3. Students will learn to take responsibility for their own learning, through active learning projects, skills workshops and information about academic support services, and participation in cocurricular programming that invites them to connect their learning inside and outside of the classroom.

The focus on questioning in the first two objectives is highly significant, and it represents an important faculty discovery: asking questions can be isolated pedagogically and can serve effectively as a novice's introduction to the larger critical thinking process.

By the end of the initial six workshops, the faculty had not only refined the course and the program in compelling ways but had also, as an unintended consequence, established a model for subsequent faculty development workshops.

Inquiry-Guided Faculty Development

If the faculty response to the steering committee's course objectives taught us that determining outcomes needed to be a collaborative venture, bringing in outside pedagogy experts taught us another key lesson: *lecturing* faculty on how to teach using inquiry-guided practices is ineffective. Among our six sessions, two featured outside experts. Both offered worthwhile know-how, the one on inspiring and evaluating student class participation, the other on constructing and employing evaluative rubrics. Yet both also tended to presume too little expertise among our own faculty.

Future workshops would succeed only if they met two conditions, each honoring the spirit of IGL at the heart of our initiative: they would need to speak to authentic faculty questions (for instance, how can we use writing exercises to help students develop analytical skills?), and they would need to engage the faculty as active sources of insight rather than as passive receptacles for knowledge. When we began to practice what we preached, our workshops became labs for our classrooms.

Subsequently, we developed an annual series of spring workshops based on issues that arose in the fall delivery of the course and in previous workshops. Instead of the big-school model in which professionals affiliated with an institutional teaching center design and facilitate workshops, we tapped primarily our own faculty to lead their peers. Our faculty led sessions on such topics as developmental learning theory, Bloom's taxonomy, teaching critical reading practices, developing problem-based learning assignments, using journal writing to promote critical reflection, teaching without talking, creating service learning projects, and structuring the exploration of academic majors as mini research projects. Each year we made sure that at least one workshop revolved around faculty sharing "assignments that really worked," inquiry-guided exercises both in and out of the classroom that engaged students while achieving at least one course objective. First-year seminar faculty were paid modest stipends to participate in these workshops, but the entire faculty was invited to attend and each year many outside the program did.

Although we have especially depended on in-house expertise, we have also continued to benefit from the occasional guest expert whose outside experience could contribute perspectives we could not supply as well on our own. We have been careful, however, to seek outside expertise only where it answered an authentic faculty need and from experts who could promise to engage our faculty in an active and collaborative workshop process.

Over the course of five years, 57 percent of our faculty have taught the freshman course and participated in workshops. Moreover, because we have also provided annual faculty-wide workshops on IGL and student engagement, practically all the faculty have participated in faculty development supporting this initiative. In addition, we created and each year have expanded a Web-based archive of inquiry-guided pedagogical strategies and exercises that instructors can draw upon. Collectively, our brand of faculty development workshops has not only reinforced the principles and habits of IGL but has also reinforced our sense of ourselves as teachers working together to become more effective.

First-Year Course Implementation and Assessment

Ultimately, the success of our program depended on arriving at consensus on the big picture while allowing flexibility in how individual faculty did their jobs.

We structured the program in relation to an annual, overarching "big question." So, for instance, one year the question was, What is normal? The course kicked off with a panel of five faculty members from different disciplines who provided seven-minute appraisals of a common reading (in this case, Mark Haddon's novel *The Curious Incident of the Dog in the Night-time*) to model how different academic disciplines focus on different problems and raise different questions. (Is the book about autism? About parenting? About rational versus emotional problem solving?) Building on "Autism, Animals, and Design," the address of the fall convocation speaker, Temple Grandin, a cocurricular program of four additional faculty panels allowed the entire freshman class to come together every few weeks to share an experience that further examined the broad common theme, exploring "normal brains," "normal beauty," normal choices," and "normal American culture." Within their own sections, instructors individualized the broad topic through such subtopics as food, American religious traditions, and the creative process. (What is normal eating? What is normal religious practice? What is normal beauty?) Students were thus invited to transfer the kind of exploration modeled in the cocurricular programming to other concrete examples.

With such a varied and wide-ranging program, we had to select wisely what we could and would assess. Although we wanted the program to help students develop critical thinking, our more particular focus on "questions that matter" reflected our judgment that a one-credit course could not change students' critical thinking ability significantly. Instead, we wanted to help shape the dispositions of our freshmen: we wanted them to see college learning as an active process that required their hands-on engagement and their disciplined attention. In other words, college learning required them to accept responsibility for their own learning. And we wanted to inspire them to exchange their expectation that good teaching consists of delivering entertaining lectures for the expectation that good teaching actually demands that they do their own thinking. In short, we wanted to prepare them to approach all of their courses with the kinds of habits and attitudes that would help them grow as learners over the long term.

Consequently, we focused our assessment on two major outcomes. First, did students perceive themselves as having absorbed the values and methods of independent, inquiry-guided learning? Course survey responses to these perceptual measures demonstrate a high level of programmatic success. More than 80 percent reported that they primarily learned by doing rather than through lecture in this course; 86 percent agreed that the course helped them understand the nature of academic inquiry and critical thinking; 77 percent agreed that this course, more than others, helped them understand how to form constructive critical questions; 77 percent also agreed that the course helped them understand ways in which different disciplines bring different kinds of questions to bear on a given issue.

The second major outcome we sought to assess was students' demonstrated ability to approach a complex problem by asking significant questions that could lead to deeper exploration and understanding. Each year, faculty have assigned a final exam question directly assessing the degree to which students could demonstrate their ability to raise critical questions in relation to one of the complex problems explored in their section. Each year we collected samples of strong, average, and weak responses from each section to gain a snapshot of what this request meant to our students and how well they succeeded in meeting our expectations of what it means to raise critical questions.

The results of this activity have been uneven and for the most part more meaningful as an assessment of how differently faculty have approached the course than of how well students can approach complex problems. For instance, one instructor asked students to interrogate the perpetrators of the genocide in Rwanda in a mock trial, and another asked students to make a list of questions that could lead them to a satisfying future career choice. Hence, from section to section student assignments were not always comparable. However, most instructors felt that the vast majority of students met at least minimal competency at this task on the final exam. Still, fall 2010 instructors in their own end-of-course survey rated only 68 percent of their students as having developed good questioning skills by the end of the semester.

Five years of experience with this program have led our faculty to three conclusions. First, emphasizing student responsibility and independent learning through an inquiry-guided approach in this course has succeeded in orienting students to the learning principles and methods we most value. Second, the program has inspired a collaboration of our faculty around delivering an education more and more authentically centered on those values. Third, the fact that 22 percent of students did not demonstrate strong critical questioning skills at the end of the course indicates that one first-semester course cannot do it alone.

Fortunately, the faculty's investment in IGL has had important curricular consequences beyond this freshman course. Inspired by our growing appreciation of the benefits of student self-directed learning, in fall 2009 Virginia Wesleyan passed a motion to transition from a three-credit course structure to a four-credit enhanced course structure. Every course will be enhanced in distinctive ways that add up to more engaged and experiential learning through active learning projects ranging from research papers to creative undertakings, service learning, and other community-based experiences. The first-year seminar course will continue to offer students their initial introduction to this model of learning, but we will formally link that course to four-credit courses that can offer students deeper introductory inquiry experiences.

In short, the faculty's own inquiry-guided exploration of IGL helped galvanize support for the adoption of a plan for comprehensive curricular reform centered on active student learning.

Conclusion

IGL requires a leap of faith from professors who believe they may even do harm by "abandoning" their students to a more independent pursuit of learning. What this approach really asks for is a terrific respect for students. It asks that we trust that, with guidance, novice learners can do for themselves what professors historically did for them: challenge received truths and investigate for themselves not only what there is to know but why and how we come to know it.

In the same way, we could not have incorporated active learning across the curriculum without having shown faculty the respect that they, too, deserve. After all, developing new approaches to teaching is time consuming and even risky compared to the model of delivering knowledge by lecture. To show faculty proper respect, we needed to provide opportunities that let them explore and pilot these ideas without implying that such new techniques were magic or that their own tried-and-true approaches were useless. In truth, to make new pedagogies work, faculty inevitably adapt and incorporate them into approaches that reflect their individual temperaments and bear their own signatures.

If we began with the premise that questions drive the most effective learning for students, we came to understand that the most effective faculty development was no different. You cannot tell students what to know and you cannot tell faculty how to teach. As we move forward in our commitment to inquiry-guided curricular reform, the question of how best to integrate abstract principles of IGL with concrete and individualized teaching practices will continue to matter.

References

Boyer Commission on Educating Undergraduates in the Research University. *Reinventing Undergraduate Education: A Blueprint for America's Research Universities.* Stony Brook: State University of New York at Stony Brook, 1998. Retrieved May 15, 2005, from http://naples.cc.sunysb.edu/Pres/boyer.nsf.

Lee, V. S., ed. *Teaching and Learning Through Inquiry: A Guidebook for Institutions and Instructors.* Sterling, Va.: Stylus, 2004.

Additional Resources

Association of American Colleges and Universities. *Greater Expectations: A New Vision for Learning as a Nation Goes to College.* Washington, D.C.: Association of American Colleges and Universities, 2002. Retrieved May 2005 from http://www.greaterexpectations.org.

Bain, K. *What the Best Colleges Do.* Cambridge: Harvard University Press, 2004.

Breivik, P. S. "21st-Century Learning and Information Literacy." *Change,* 2005, 37(2), 20–27.

Diestler, S. *Becoming a Critical Thinker,* 4th ed. Upper Saddle River, N.J.: Pearson/Prentice Hall, 2005.

John N. Gardner Institute for Excellence in Undergraduate Education. "Publications."
Retrieved Dec. 8, 2011, from http://www.jngi.org/research-publications/publications.
Paul, R., and L. Elder. Various resources in critical thinking available from the
Foundation for Critical Thinking, at www.criticalthinking.org.
Perry, W. *Forms of Intellectual and Ethical Development in the College Years—A Scheme.*
San Francisco: Jossey-Bass, 1999.
Sellen, M. "Information Literacy in the General Education: A New Requirement for the
21st Century." *Journal of General Education,* 2002, 51(2), 115–26.

*LISA CARSTENS is professor of English and associate dean of the college at
Virginia Wesleyan College, as well as an instructor of first-year seminar.
During the implementation of this QEP, she served as associate dean of inquiry-
guided learning and director of the QEP, with primary oversight of the new
first-year seminar program and leadership of the curriculum reform initiative.*

*JOYCE BERNSTEIN HOWELL is professor of art history at Virginia Wesleyan
College, as well as an instructor of first-year seminar. She chaired the committee that wrote the inquiry-guided learning QEP (2005), and thereafter served in
the series of committees leading to curricular reform. She is currently cochair
of the task force for the SACS fifth-year interim report, which includes assessment of the QEP.*

6

*This chapter describes the initiative designed to transform the
largest enrollment classes at Miami University to focus on
inquiry-guided learning and student engagement and discusses
the results thus far.*

Integrating Inquiry-Guided Learning Across the Curriculum: The Top 25 Project at Miami University

*Beverley A. P. Taylor, Andrea I. Bakker, Marjorie Keeshan Nadler,
Cecilia Shore, Beth Dietz-Uhler*

In 2006, Miami University (Oxford, Ohio) launched a major initiative, the Top 25 Project, to embed inquiry-guided learning (IGL) into our largest-enrollment courses across the university. These are generally entry-level classes and thus affect many students: 75 percent of incoming students on our main campus in 2010 were in at least one Top 25 class. The initiative began at the highest level of administration and was informed by student intellectual development theory and research. Our president and his collaborators outlined a "student as scholar" model in which educators "help students become more internally focused by validating them as thinkers and burgeoning scholars, presenting thorny problems and topics that lend themselves to multiple legitimate perspectives, introducing them to competencies needed to address those topics, and helping them form, and accept responsibility for, their own decisions and actions" (Hodge, Baxter Magolda, and Haynes, 2009, 19). The Top 25 Project was the first step in infusing this model into the university culture.

Until the Top 25 Project, IGL at Miami (as at many other institutions) was used sporadically in some disciplines, often in senior-level classes, but it was not a widespread approach. To make an impact on student conceptions of learning early in their university experience, we targeted courses that most students take in their first two years. We believed that IGL would

NEW DIRECTIONS FOR TEACHING AND LEARNING, no. 129, Spring 2012 © Wiley Periodicals, Inc.
Published online in Wiley Online Library (wileyonlinelibrary.com) • DOI: 10.1002/tl.20007

61

provide both the support and structure that beginning college students need. Courses for beginning students also tend to have large enrollments and thus reach the student body broadly. The 25 largest enrollment courses were targeted to participate in a curriculum development project, although 27 courses are currently participating. As expected, these courses were primarily disciplinary survey courses in our general education curriculum. However, about one-third of the courses were second- and third-year courses in our Farmer School of Business that form the core courses required of all business majors.

To provide support and feedback to faculty as they redesigned and piloted their courses, initiation was staggered over four years with four to seven courses launched each year. Faculty teams were funded for two years to redesign the pedagogy of their courses around IGL and other active learning strategies. The first teams began in the spring of 2007 and the last in the spring of 2010. To use active learning and IGL to increase the depth of critical thinking, faculty were encouraged to move low-level memory-based learning outside of the classroom allowing valuable classroom time to be used for higher-level activities in which the engagement of faculty and students is essential. This change also increased the engagement of students with their peers both in and out of the classroom and increased the amount of time devoted to learning outside of the classroom.

Each team had different needs, so support varied according to the discipline and the nature of the proposed course redesign. Discipline-specific external consultants were brought in for some teams. Most teams, however, drew on support from our instructional technology team, writing center staff, library staff, and Center for the Enhancement of Learning, Teaching, and University Assessment staff. The Top 25 administrative team (predominantly faculty with expertise in IGL and assessment) consulted with each team and offered ongoing feedback.

Because many of our faculty were not familiar with IGL, we (the Top 25 administrative team) convened a seminar to explore IGL with the first set of course team leaders. We began with the definition of IGL drawn from Virginia Lee's (2004, p. 9) book: "an array of classroom practices that promote student learning through guided and increasingly, independent investigation of complex questions and problems, often for which there is no single answer." Because IGL is grounded in the scholarship of a discipline, it may mean different things in different disciplinary contexts. The group read broadly about how IGL has been used in a variety of disciplines (for example, Brooking, 1995; Minstrell and van Zee, 2000; Plowright and Watkins, 2004; and Justice, Rice, Warry, and Laurie, 2007). Faculty were encouraged to choose a model of IGL that worked best for their own discipline. In the sciences this involved asking questions and collecting evidence in the laboratory. In the fine arts the focus was on how and why artists create their work. In the School of Business, inquiry centered on decision making in realistic scenarios.

NEW DIRECTIONS FOR TEACHING AND LEARNING • DOI: 10.1002/tl

Near the end of the seminar, we asked team leaders to write descriptions of IGL in their own field. The following responses provide some sense of the breadth and depth of their thinking.

"Inquiry-based learning asks students to be actively engaged with both disciplinary material and the learning process, and it requires trial and error on the part of students to be successful. It switches the educational focus from what a teacher is doing to students to what teachers are doing with students and what students are doing with each other and the world around them." Professor Nadler, Communication

"In inquiry-based learning in human geography, students express their curiosity by critically exploring the local and global transformations that shape the world they live in and will inherit. Engaged students of human geography thus learn firsthand how to act as informed and committed global citizens." Professor Prytherch, Geography

"Inquiry-based learning in the sciences provides students an opportunity to see science as process of interrogating nature rather than a collection of facts to be learned. Students will explore central concepts by manipulating materials, making observations and looking for patterns, developing explanatory models and testing predictions." Professor Taylor, Physics

"To me, inquiry-based learning occurs when students discover the important concepts in a discipline themselves. Instead of providing the information in a class, the instructor guides students as they learn on their own." Professor Butler, Art

"Using an onion analogy, instead of us peeling away the onion for them (when they may not even understand the concept of onion), we get them interested in the onion enough to want to peel it themselves and support them in that peeling process." Professor Benamati, Management Information Systems

"The goal is to prepare learners to become curious about the world in which they live, and empower them to become independent learners eager to discover answers to those questions using appropriate scholarly/scientific methods. Those answers should lead students to ask new questions and initiate new inquiries." Professor Mark, Psychology

The Courses

The Top 25 courses have instantiated their definitions of IGL in different ways. One reason for the differences has been the traditional pedagogies employed by different disciplines, sometimes referred to as "signature pedagogies" (Shulman, 2005), such as lecture-lab combinations in the sciences. Other differences have arisen due to staffing constraints, such as a large number of sections led by part-time instructors. Some of the differences have arisen because different teams emphasized different desired qualities for Top 25 classes.

Several of the courses have been revised to emphasize inquiry defined as participating in the discipline as it is actually practiced. The Department of Theater previously had a traditional theater appreciation course that focused on theater history. Their revision transformed the course to center on how theater productions are created. Over the semester students were exposed to practitioners of various theater components, such as costuming, lighting, staging, and acting. In small groups, they produced and performed their own short pieces. Similarly, the Department of Psychology changed the focus of their class from a survey of topics to exercises in how psychologists use evidence.

Our Top 25 chemistry and biology courses revised their laboratory sections. Traditionally these have focused on verifications of principles taught in lecture. The redesigns take a variety of approaches. Sometimes they introduce students to a concept before it is addressed in lecture. At other times they pose a question and the point of the lab is to design an experiment that would answer the question. Classmates critique the solutions, modeling for students the peer review process typical of scientific inquiry. Sometimes, real-life problems are posed, such as analyzing locally collected water samples for various chemicals.

Technology has enabled students in some courses to receive practice and feedback in discipline-specific skills. For example, our management course has adopted software called "Virtual Leader" that allows students to try out various solutions to management problems in organizations and observe the effects of different leadership decisions. Our communication course uses software that allows faculty to video students giving a speech and simultaneously post it on a Web site for students to play back for self-assessment. Another piece of software prepares students for the often dreaded impromptu speech. The software generates topics, records and times the student's speech, and allows the student to review it. With practice their confidence improves.

Some course revisions focus on inquiry defined as student engagement with applications of the material. One method to heighten student in-class involvement is referred to as the "inverted classroom" (Lage, Platt, and Treglia, 2000). This technique moves lower-level learning out of the classroom; instructors post lectures as videos to be viewed before class. Class time is spent doing group work on case studies and other applied problems, so the support of peers and the instructor is available when the students need it. Some large lecture classes did not move completely to an inverted classroom model but now feature more in-class interaction, with short lectures interspersed with small group activities, think-pair-share dialogues, and clicker questions.

In some cases, especially ones involving multiple instructors (for example, communication and calculus classes), the team created a variety of IGL options that individual faculty could draw on in redesigning their class. This modular approach supports faculty autonomy and enables the course to evolve through the creativity of new contributions.

Other teams enhanced their large lecture classes by adding breakout sections for discussions. In itself this is not unusual, but the psychology department took the additional step of having these sections led by trained undergraduate discussion leaders. By engaging in the academic practice of teaching, the undergraduate leaders gain a new perspective on their own education. The culminating course in the training sequence for undergraduate teaching assistants encourages them to carry out their own pedagogical inquiry project.

Assessment

Assessment of the Top 25 Project goals was an essential part of the project. The departments focused on assessing students' mastery of the course content, whereas the administrative team focused on the broader goals of the project such as increased time spent in class on inquiry (with a subsequent decrease in time spent on low-level material), improved critical thinking, and increased student satisfaction. The administrative team used a variety of formative assessment methods, including student focus groups and classroom observations, and summative methods, including end-of-semester surveys and assessments of student writing samples.

The formative assessments provided detailed feedback about a course to the individual instructors and department. Because of the highly individualized focus of these methods, neither the classroom observations nor the focus groups were intended to provide feedback about the project as a whole. There are no formal data that indicate how effective these methods were in terms of improving courses, although individual instructors have indicated they appreciated the feedback and made changes as a result.

Course observations were conducted by a member of the administrative team using a protocol that identified types of inquiry-guided activities for which to look. Each observer later met with the instructor to discuss the extent to which the course was achieving the goals of the Top 25 Project as well as methods for encouraging students to be more actively involved in their learning.

Student focus groups provided detailed feedback to instructors and teams about students' perceptions of the course, specific activities within the course, and the extent to which the course encouraged IGL. The forty-five- to sixty-minute focus groups were conducted outside of the classroom by two administrative team members. The open-ended nature of the focus groups elicited useful feedback that confirmed and at times explained the results of some of the other assessment methods as well as offered insight into the different IGL methods employed in each class.

The end-of-semester surveys and assessments of student writing samples provided summative assessments of the Top 25 Project. The results of these assessments were shared with instructors and individual departments; data from all of the courses were combined to provide information about the progress of the project as a whole. The surveys assessed students' general satisfaction with the course, the extent to which the course used inquiry and active learning, the amount and type of critical thinking activities in which students participated, the extent to which students engaged with other learners, and the extent to which low-level learning (such as memorization) had been shifted from inside of the classroom to outside of the classroom and replaced with more challenging activities (such as analysis and synthesis).

The surveys included only closed-ended questions and were distributed during the last month of the semester. The majority of students completed the surveys online and outside of the classroom, although a small number of instructors opted to distribute the survey during class time (either on paper or online). When possible the survey was distributed to both traditional and redesigned sections of a course. For some courses traditional data were not collected because the department made changes to the course immediately upon acceptance into the Top 25 Project.

Although the surveys and student focus groups provided a wealth of information about students' perceptions of the course, neither provided direct information on students' achievement of the specified learning outcomes. To fill this need, direct assessments of student writing were conducted. Team leaders, in collaboration with Top 25 administrative staff, identified one or more written projects that were designed to elicit critical thinking from the students and designed a rubric that was used to assess the level of critical thinking demonstrated in the assignment. A group of Miami faculty trained in assessing critical thinking used the rubrics to assess the student work. The results of the writing sample assessments were provided to instructors with the goal of encouraging them to improve assignments so that they required more critical thinking, made expectations clearer to students, and revised teaching practices to enhance critical thinking. We are currently in the process of analyzing several years of data to look for evidence of change in critical thinking ability.

Results

Overall, the end-of-semester survey results suggest that students perceive the redesigned courses to include more IGL, to be more engaging, to involve more critical thinking, and to be more effortful than traditional versions of the course. The biggest difference between redesigned and traditional versions of the course was student perceptions of engagement. All differences between the traditional course and the redesigned course are statistically significant, suggesting that students perceive the redesigned courses to be meeting the goals of the Top 25 program.

There is also anecdotal data to corroborate these results. For example, students in an introductory theater course were asked to describe their experiences in the course, indicating how the course did or did not use IGL. Student comments included:

> "We took learning into our hands, set our own goals, and explored our own ideas. There was no definite answer; we had to investigate and figure it out for ourselves."

> "We were trusted with class time to lead our own learning for the day."

> "We had to think for ourselves and see other people's perspectives."

> "The instructor helped us think through issues without telling the answer. He made us *want* to think."

These comments clearly indicate that students are beginning to take ownership of and responsibility for their own learning. They also indicate that students appreciate the value of IGL.

It is interesting to note that faculty are seeing a transformation in their students, particularly in the School of Business in which many core courses are Top 25 classes. For example, in a recent marketing department faculty meeting, changes in students in their upper-level classes were noted, which they attribute to students having taken Top 25 courses. They report that students in their classes:

- Are more willing to take risks
- Are thinking collaboratively
- Are more capable of analytical thinking
- Display more imagination
- Are more willing to come to the instructor with questions

All of these results suggest that students are benefiting in important ways from an inquiry-guided approach.

Challenges and Rewards

As with any large curriculum project, there have been and will continue to be challenges. Periodic team leader meetings were valuable in allowing teams to discuss issues and progress as well as draw on the experience of each other and prior teams. For example, some teams were focused on how to move lower-level learning outside the class while still holding students responsible. The early adopters reported what they had tried, modified, and ultimately were using, saving trial and error time for those who followed. Thus, the learning community created by the program helped to share ideas, approaches, and strategies.

Faculty motivation for participation in the program was uneven. Some faculty were enthusiastic about embracing the IGL model whereas others were more resistant to calls for change. However, faculty motivation was enhanced by the team approach, the flexibility given to each discipline to approach the course redesign in the manner best suited to the nature of their class, and the consistent support offered by the core Top 25 team and the additional support staff. In fact, some faculty who were resistant at the outset are excited by the changes they see occurring in their classrooms. In a recent survey of Top 25 Project faculty, about 75 percent of faculty who taught Top 25 redesigned courses reported that they perceived that student engagement and learning had increased as a result of the redesign. In addition, more than two-thirds reported that they enjoyed teaching the redesigned course more than the traditional course.

Students were also resistant initially to the additional work and expectations placed upon them by the redesigned approach. Some students had not developed the skills needed to critically read texts on their own and abstract key information, so support needed to be built into some classes to help develop these skills. Students often found that the additional thinking and work were hard. In addition, students had previously approached group work by dividing the work into individual units rather than the true collaboration that was called for by the IGL models. International students in particular had some special challenges in adapting to the expectations of the new model when it did not fit well with their prior experiences. Over time and with the larger number of classes altering student roles, students have new expectations for the classes as the new learning culture takes hold for both faculty and students.

Higher administration support for course changes was critically important to the successful adoption of the IGL models. These approaches required more faculty time and often resulted in initially lowered course evaluations. Administrative support was necessary at all levels, including department chairs, deans, and provost, to reassure faculty that this was valued and would be taken into account in tenure, promotion, and merit raise contexts.

The Top 25 program faces challenges in sustaining the advances generated by these efforts. There is ongoing turnover among faculty and administrative leadership. Newcomers need to be trained on an ongoing basis, and the courses themselves need to continue to evolve and grow within the inquiry-guided learning framework. Many of the changes started on the main campus and the need for adoption on regional campuses require ongoing communication, clear priorities, and adequate support. There are also ongoing costs associated with many of the new designs as software needs to be updated and equipment becomes worn out or outdated. Many classes have needed three to four years of work before faculty and students became comfortable with the revised approach, and ongoing assessment methods are necessary for that time period to ensure the redesigned classes are sustained.

Despite the challenges faced in sustaining the initiative, there is evidence that IGL has taken hold and that a culture shift is occurring throughout the university. Survey evidence suggests classes that are not part of the Top 25 program are starting to embrace more inquiry-guided models and enhanced student engagement. New university initiatives have also been developed around the IGL approach championed by the Top 25 program. For example, psychology has started a program targeted at upward integration of the approaches throughout the curriculum as a next step. A First-Year Research Experience program was launched to help support first-year students engaging in research rather than emphasizing seniors as prior projects have done. These and similar advances have made it clear that the large scale Top 25 Project has served as a catalyst for change.

References

Brooking, D. "Putting a Mustache on the *Mona Lisa*: Violating Expectations in Teaching." *Journal on Excellence in College Teaching*, 1995, 6(2), 79–97.

Hodge, D. C., M. B. Baxter Magolda, and C. A. Haynes. "Engaged Learning: Enabling Self-Authorship and Effective Practice." *Liberal Education*, 2009, 95(4), 16–23.

Justice, C., J. Rice, W. Warry, and I. Laurie. "Taking an 'Inquiry' Course Makes a Difference: A Comparative Analysis of Student Learning." *Journal on Excellence in College Teaching*, 2007, 18(1), 57–77.

Lage, M., G. Platt, and M. Treglia. "Inverting the Classroom: A Gateway to Creating an Inclusive Learning Environment." *Journal of Economics Education*, 2000, 31(1), 30–43.

Lee, V. S., ed. *Teaching and Learning Through Inquiry: A Guidebook for Institutions and Instructors*. Sterling, Va.: Stylus Publishing, 2004.

Minstrell, J., and E. van Zee, eds. *Inquiry into Inquiry Learning and Teaching in Science*. Washington, D.C.: American Association for the Advancement of Science, 2000.

Plowright, D., and M. Watkins. "There Are No Problems to Be Solved, Only Inquiries to Be Made, in Social Work Education." *Innovation in Education and Teaching International*, 2004, 41(2), 185–206.

Shulman, L. S. "Signature Pedagogies in the Professions." *Daedalus*, 2005, 134(3), 52–59.

BEVERLEY A. P. TAYLOR is a professor in the Department of Physics and director of the Top 25 Project at Miami University. She has expertise in inquiry-guided learning, assessment, and faculty development and has been involved in the Top 25 Project since its inception.

ANDREA I. BAKKER is the assistant director of institutional research. She has served as an assessment consultant on the Top 25 administrative team and also sat on the committee that reviewed Top 25 proposals.

MARJORIE KEESHAN NADLER is a professor in the Department of Communication, was a team leader for a first-round class, and is a faculty associate with the Top 25 program.

CECILIA SHORE is director of the Center for the Enhancement of Learning, Teaching, and University Assessment and has participated in proposal review, led focus groups, assessed critical thinking papers, and worked with university administrators to support and promote the Top 25 Project.

BETH DIETZ-UHLER is a professor in the Department of Psychology, a team member for a first-round class, and an assessment associate with the Top 25 Project.

7

This chapter describes the creation, implementation, and assessment of a systematic program of inquiry-guided learning and discusses some of the challenges posed.

Marymount University: Inquiry-Guided Learning as a Catalyst for Change

Carolyn Oxenford, Liane Summerfield, Michael Schuchert

Introduction

Marymount University is a midsized, independent Catholic university whose mission combines a liberal arts foundation with career preparation and opportunities for personal and professional development. The university is moderately selective with a highly diverse undergraduate student population. Approximately half of Marymount undergraduates are transfer students.

In 2007, as a component of reaffirmation of its accreditation by the Southern Association of Colleges and Schools-Commission on Colleges (SACS-COC), the university community selected integrating research across the undergraduate curriculum as its quality enhancement plan (QEP). This topic was driven by the university's mission as a student-centered learning community that values diversity and focuses on educating the whole person.

The QEP planning committee knew that Marymount students needed classroom experiences that would develop the skills, attitudes, and habits of independent thinking required for successful research. Inquiry-guided learning (IGL) was a perfect fit and became a central component of the QEP. This chapter describes program development, implementation, and assessment activities and our current challenges to date.

Development of the DISCOVER Program

Marymount's QEP is titled "DISCOVER: Inquiry, Scholarship, Creativity, and Research." DISCOVER's mission is to promote student engagement in learning communities at Marymount and in national and international settings, through research, creative work, and IGL. The QEP addresses academic excellence, engagement, and student retention by supporting an active-learning environment in which stronger students can meet new challenges and struggling students are identified early and supported.

Choosing a model of IGL that fit the needs of disciplines ranging from philosophy to fashion design was important to the development of DISCOVER. Lee's definition of IGL as "an array of classroom practices that promote student learning through guided and increasingly independent investigation of complex questions and problems, often for which there is no single answer" (Lee, 2004, p. 9) was sufficiently broad for our purposes. This definition along with Hudspith and Jenkins' (2001) inquiry process and Justice (2006) inquiry outcomes were shared with faculty across the university. Faculty were encouraged to adapt these models to their favored disciplinary modes of inquiry, for example, problem solving, empirical, research from sources, or performance.

As we continued to refine DISCOVER and develop our assessment process, we came to appreciate the developmental nature of inquiry skills and attitudes. The Research Skill Development (RSD) framework (Willison and O'Regan, 2007) helped us conceptualize the development of inquiry skills from first year though graduation and beyond and informed the development of our inquiry rubric, the Discover Assessment Tool, described later in this chapter.

Components of DISCOVER

DISCOVER includes a series of interlocking initiatives designed to refocus the undergraduate curriculum to include IGL and research. These are summarized next and outlined in Table 7.1.

First-Year Seminar. A new three-credit first-year seminar provides a foundation in IGL and integrates students into the university community. Four sections of the seminar (DSC101) were piloted in fall 2008 and ten sections in fall 2009. Beginning in fall 2010, the course was required for all first-year students.

Each DSC101 instructor incorporates his or her chosen theme into common course outcomes. Students select inquiry topics; develop plans and goals for inquiry; gather and analyze necessary information; demonstrate oral communication skills in presenting inquiry results; and write accurate, clear, and coherent summaries of results. Each course section has a peer mentor who supports student adjustment and helps implement inquiry-guided projects.

NEW DIRECTIONS FOR TEACHING AND LEARNING • DOI: 10.1002/tl

Table 7.1. Inquiry-Guided Learning in the DISCOVER Program

Elements	Direct involvement in inquiry-guided learning	Supportive of inquiry-guided learning
Required	• DSC101 First-Year Seminar OR • DSC201 City as Inquiry (transfer seminar) • Inquiry courses in the majors (200, 300, and capstone)	• Liberal Arts Core competencies (students) • DSC101 training (faculty)
Optional	Student-faculty research opportunities	• DISCOVER Center support services • Faculty development activities • Faculty research grants • Participation in Student Research Conference

Transfer Seminar. A one-credit transfer seminar (DSC201) will be piloted in fall 2011 with four sections. DSC201: City as Inquiry will introduce new transfer students to Marymount University and to IGL, using the Washington metropolitan area's rich resources. This course will prepare transfer students for upper-level inquiry courses in their majors, and particularly for their capstone projects. It also will provide a baseline measure of students' inquiry skills upon entering the university.

Refocused Undergraduate Curriculum. All degree-granting programs have identified required major courses that will use IGL. At least one 200-level course and one 300-level course in each major includes inquiry outcomes and assignments, as well as an inquiry-guided capstone experience. To provide some consistency across disciplines, these inquiry courses use the Hudspith and Jenkins (2001) framework of exploring, defining a central question, developing a strategy, executing the strategy, critically assessing outcomes, drawing conclusions, and communicating one's findings. In addition, all inquiry courses have a required individual inquiry product that is assessed using a common rubric. Syllabi for inquiry courses must be approved by the DISCOVER faculty advisory group, using a rubric that assesses required inquiry components.

Undergraduate Research Center. The DISCOVER program has expanded extracurricular undergraduate research opportunities for students in several ways. A summer program for students and faculty mentors working together on research or creative endeavors began in summer 2009. The program includes stipends for students and mentors and for student room and board. An online directory of faculty mentors was created to assist students in locating research opportunities at the university, and additional off-campus research internships have been identified. Increased funding for student research and travel to conferences is available, and the annual student research conference has been expanded to allow for enhanced celebration of student work.

Core Curriculum Integration. IGL also is integrated into Marymount's revised (2007–08) liberal arts core curriculum as a core competency. The Liberal Arts Core also includes competencies in several skill areas that support undergraduate research and IGL, including critical thinking, communication, and information literacy. A library specialist in information literacy works with DISCOVER, and a writing specialist position was added in 2009–10.

Embracing Inquiry-Guided Instruction

Although most members of the QEP design committee were faculty and the entire faculty voted to approve the project, it was clear that many faculty would need help embracing IGL. The Center for Teaching Excellence (CTE) approached this challenge developmentally. The CTE director arranged for two full days of faculty development with Virginia Lee in spring 2008 to introduce IGL and to provide an opportunity to ask questions and discuss how IGL could fit into existing courses and programs. This training was available to full-time and adjunct faculty. Academic administrators also had the opportunity to discuss the implications of incorporating IGL into their programs.

After this introduction, each of the four academic schools was offered a specialized faculty development program for the entire school. Two schools chose this approach and the others took an individual route. A session on IGL required for full-time faculty was held during the following fall semester faculty convocation. These faculty development sessions did not focus on specific courses but on IGL in general.

Support for DSC101. Two 2-hour summer training workshops were held each year for faculty selected to teach DSC101 sections. These workshops focused on characteristics of first-year students, practical advice about course logistics, and support for designing and implementing inquiry projects. The participants experienced and debriefed an inquiry-guided exercise and shared plans for their classes. The CTE director and DISCOVER director scheduled lunch meetings for DSC101 faculty to discuss successes and concerns while they were teaching the course, which provided another opportunity to identify needs and share strategies. The CTE and DISCOVER directors offer ongoing information sessions for current and prospective DSC101 faculty in August, October, and January during regularly scheduled faculty development events. Most of these events are open to adjunct as well as full-time faculty.

Support for Curricular Reform. Required inquiry courses were added to the majors in fall 2010. Faculty development for these disciplinary-based inquiry courses has been less comprehensive, particularly among adjunct faculty. Although some adjuncts have taught DSC101 and participated in that training, adjuncts who are teaching in the disciplines generally have not participated in faculty development; this is a source of concern. The CTE director is working to develop an IGL tutorial that could be placed online, particularly for adjunct faculty.

In addition to specific faculty support for IGL, Marymount now sends faculty to conferences and workshops focusing on best teaching practices, including Fink's Integrated Course Design, Association of American Colleges and Universities (AACU) team events, University of Delaware case-based teaching workshops, Ken Bain's summer workshop, and the Tidewater Consortium summer program. Even though these programs may not focus on IGL, they serve to introduce faculty to learner-centered teaching, an important step in the process of becoming an effective inquiry-guided instructor. The CTE attempts to match faculty readiness with the characteristics of these programs so that faculty are challenged and refreshed by their experiences. Afterward, faculty attendees provide workshops or information sessions for their peers to share what they have learned, and some have become "missionaries" to departments where IGL is not firmly established. The CTE and the provost also have offered summer course redesign stipends for faculty who want to incorporate innovative pedagogical approaches to specific courses, and beginning in fall 2010 they are offering course releases for similar purposes. Having a wide range of incentives and supports allows us to reward and develop our enthusiastic early adopters as well as to engage our late bloomers.

Implementing Inquiry-Guided Learning in the Disciplines

The combination of DISCOVER and the Liberal Arts Core revisions has sparked curricular innovations in many departments at Marymount. As is typical with curricular reform on this scale, some departments have embraced IGL with more enthusiasm and success than others, although all departments have experienced some level of change.

The Health Sciences program has embraced IGL and used it to transform several courses. This program prepares students for graduate study or careers in health and fitness fields. According to the department chairperson, Mike Nordvall, developing inquiry courses has been a natural fit for his discipline, which has always had a significant skills component. In addition to traditional skills training, the department's inquiry courses now use case study methodology and have reduced or eliminated lecture. Nordvall identified two areas that have proved challenging in shifting to inquiry-guided instruction. The first is giving up the sense of control that lecture-based teaching imparts. His other major concern has been student resistance to inquiry-guided methods. Students in his program have needed repeated, explicit information regarding the benefits of IGL compared to traditional lectures. The need for explicit discussions of the nature and value of IGL has been noted by other faculty as well.

The Mathematics department at Marymount has begun to incorporate inquiry into their program despite initial concerns about reducing lecture and classroom demonstration. Assistant professor Laurie Lenz was inspired by the institutional support for IGL to pursue her interest in redesigning the department's entry-level problem-solving course. She is using the Process Oriented Guided Inquiry Learning model to develop the activities she needs to transform the course. Although she is still refining the course, she already feels that the shift has been worthwhile. Dr. Lenz indicated that she would probably not have attempted inquiry-guided instruction without institutional support and the impetus of DISCOVER.

The Literature and Languages department has taken a uniquely departmental approach to adopting inquiry-guided pedagogy. Their approach has been to identify a departmental inquiry objective that is included in all of their inquiry courses: "Students will conduct appropriate research and synthesize their own original ideas with those advanced by literary critics and other scholars" (Marguerite Rippy, e-mail message, Jan. 26, 2011). Crafting this objective generated a healthy departmental conversation about the meaning of research and inquiry in their discipline. The resulting objective leaves room for nontraditional forms including interviews, oral history, digital humanities projects, and performance analyses although still providing an overarching goal of critical analysis and synthesis. Once this overall goal was established, the department focused on bringing different methods of research into each course, depending on its content area and approach. The department also adopted a standard short reflection essay component for student projects. In these essays, students discuss the research process, new strategies they tried, what worked for them, and what they would do differently in the future. This reflection requirement has been effective both for increasing student understanding of the inquiry process and for assessment of students, and we now suggest (strongly) that all inquiry courses include such a reflective component with final student projects.

Observing the varied ways that Marymount faculty are working to incorporate IGL into their courses and programs has catalyzed the development of the DISCOVER program as a whole. For example, the reflection requirement from Literature and Languages is being used in many courses to help students better understand the purpose of IGL, which helps reduce the resistance noted by faculty in Health and Human Performance. The progress in Mathematics reflects the importance of institution-wide support and commitment to inquiry-guided pedagogy. The importance of DSC101 is underscored by comments from faculty teaching upper-level inquiry courses about the need for students to be exposed to inquiry-guided methods as early as possible.

New Directions for Teaching and Learning • DOI: 10.1002/tl

Demonstrating the Effectiveness of DISCOVER

As a university initiative with planned outcomes spanning the institution, assessment of DISCOVER required a wide range of measures targeting both student achievement and institutional impact. The approach also needed to provide both formative data to ensure effective implementation and summative data to allow for a meaningful five-year follow-up report to SACS-COC.

Being mindful that assessment can be expensive and require substantial time and energy to implement, Marymount's assessment team began with existing instruments such as its annual alumni survey, the National Survey of Student Engagement (NSSE), and standardized measures like retention, which provided baseline data for several core indicators. When existing evaluation tools failed to meet DISCOVER's assessment needs, the team developed new tools and incorporated them into existing assessment processes to enhance rather than reinvent the wheel.

Assessing Student Learning. The primary direct measure for assessing students' growth as inquiry learners, the DISCOVER Assessment Tool (DAT), is a home-grown, developmentally based rubric modeled after several of AACU's VALUE rubrics (Association of American Colleges and Universities, n.d.); Bowling Green State University's Hypothesized Developmental Sequence Rubrics for Assessing Inquiry (2006); and the University of Adelaide's RSD Framework (Willison & O'Regan, 2007). Faculty use the DAT to evaluate student inquiry skills during Marymount's annual assessment workshop, which also examines liberal arts core skills such as writing, critical thinking, and information literacy. By integrating these two assessment processes, Marymount avoids duplicating efforts and generates complementary data for validating the DAT. Faculty members use the rubric to evaluate approximately eighty student papers on ten inquiry skills. Initial assessments have focused on differences between students who participated in DSC101 and those who did not. Now that all incoming students enroll in DSC101, the assessment will focus on evaluating students' development over time by assessing performance in sophomore, junior, and senior courses.

Marymount uses two primary indirect assessment tools. The *Student Inquiry Skills and Attitudes Questionnaire* (SISAQ) is a self-assessment of student confidence in core inquiry skills. We administer the tool early and late in DSC101 to measure change over the course. Like the DAT, initial analyses focused on differences between students who enrolled in DSC101 and those who did not. Now we will examine differences over time as the first full class of DSC101 students moves into upper division courses. Other indirect measures are drawn from the NSSE. Comparing local NSSE results to national norms has strengthened its usefulness as an indirect measure. We intend to model assessment of transfer student achievement using the DSC101 model and will use DSC201 as a gateway for collecting entry data.

Assessing Institutional Impact. Evaluating the impact of DISCOVER on the institution required the use of broad-focus measures such as retention and progression to graduate studies. Marymount has long struggled with retention issues and hoped that engaging students early with IGL would strengthen student retention. Institutional comfort and ease of tracking retention make it a useful and powerful measure. Measuring increases in undergraduates moving directly into graduate school has been straightforward because Marymount already tracked educational and occupational outcomes of graduates through the annual alumni survey.

To evaluate teaching changes, student course evaluations were revised to include supplemental questions focused specifically on the use of inquiry-guided pedagogy. In fall 2010 we introduced a new end-of-semester survey in DSC101 that asked about pedagogical methods in all of the students' courses. Together these administrative measures provide a picture of how inquiry is taking root at the institution.

Initial Assessment Results

Assessment findings during the pilot first semester experience showed substantial promise. Students enrolling in DSC101 were significantly stronger at developing and implementing an analysis plan than their colleagues who had not enrolled, and they showed significant increases in confidence over the course of their initial semester. The pilot students reported more engagement in inquiry activities and scored higher on all NSSE benchmarks except Supportive Campus Environment. They had a higher fall-to-spring retention rate (92 percent) compared to those participating in the traditional freshman experience (86 percent).

In the second year, the program started to show signs of losing its initial impact. Although students continued to experience a significant increase in confidence during the first semester, the differences between those participating in DSC101 and traditional seminars disappeared. The difference in fall-to-spring retention rate dropped from six points to three. Although data suggested that the program continued to have a positive impact on students, these decreases are the focus of current attention. Data from the first year of full implementation are not yet available.

Assessment results have been valuable guides during the implementation of DISCOVER. Students' relative strengths and weaknesses have shaped faculty development planning. Inconsistencies in assessment results between student perceptions and performance have underscored the importance of being explicit about the inquiry process for students. When applying the DAT to visually based projects, it became clear that students needed to include a written reflection describing the inquiry processes they used. Finally, the finding that DSC101 students did not find Marymount as supportive as those in traditional freshman seminar led to an expansion of the peer mentor role to ensure that student development elements of the traditional experience were not lost.

Challenges to DISCOVER

Assessing a new program like DISCOVER has presented both expected and unexpected challenges. The first expected challenge was developing a direct measure of IGL that faculty would support, which was complicated by the wide range of disciplines at Marymount. The assessment tools themselves provided unexpected psychometric challenges. For example, students rated their confidence levels so highly that we needed to expand the SISAQ scale from a five-point scale to a seven-point scale to measure later increases. Another unforeseen challenge associated with DISCOVER's assessment process emerged more recently. The original assessment plan had short- and long-term goals but failed to address assessment needs during years two and three. This has resulted in an "assessment donut hole," which Marymount is currently filling with new survey tools such as the end-of-semester survey and more in-depth analysis of data.

As with any innovative practice, there are early adopters and late bloomers. Marymount has benefited from strong programs in design, which routinely uses IGL, and from our physical therapy graduate program, which uses problem-based learning throughout the curriculum. At the other extreme are programs where faculty members believe they are using IGL because they ask questions in class and assign a term paper. Faculty resistance to change in some programs is still evident. One benefit of our institutional commitment to IGL is that our provost now routinely asks job candidates about their experience and commitment to active IGL. This approach has already affected faculty involvement in IGL as the cohort of inquiry-friendly faculty continues to grow. We also have started to publicize and reward programs and courses that use inquiry-guided instruction. These activities, along with ongoing faculty development, are helping us build a critical mass of faculty who are committed to IGL.

The systematic infusion of IGL and research into Marymount's undergraduate program has sparked a slow but growing shift in our culture. Fed by accreditation requirements, strong institutional support, and effective assessment, the sparks are spreading and growing among faculty and students alike into a richer and more exciting curriculum.

References

Association of American Colleges and Universities. VALUE Rubrics. n.d. Retrieved June 15, 2009, from http://www.aacu.org/value/rubrics/index.cfm.

Bowling Green State University. BGSU University Learning Outcomes. 2006. Retrieved November 15, 2011, from http://www.bgsu.edu/offices/ir/page17385.html.

Hudspith, B., and H. Jenkins. *Teaching the Art of Inquiry.* Halifax, Nova Scotia: Society for Teaching and Learning in Higher Education, 2001.

Justice, C., "Inquiry in Higher Education: Reflections and Directions on Course Design and Teaching Methods." *Innovative Higher Education,* 2006, *31,* 201–214.

Lee, V. S., ed. *Teaching and Learning Through Inquiry: A Guidebook for Institutions and Instructors.* Sterling, Va.: Stylus, 2004.

Willison, J., and K. O'Regan. Research Skill Development Framework, 2007. Retrieved July 15, 2008, from http://www.adelaide.edu.au/clpd/rsd/framework/.

CAROLYN OXENFORD *is the director of the Center for Teaching Excellence at Marymount University and a professor of psychology.*

LIANE SUMMERFIELD *is associate vice-president for academic affairs and director of the DISCOVER program. She is a professor of health and nutrition.*

MICHAEL SCHUCHERT *is the executive director for institutional effectiveness at Marymount and also serves as a regular reviewer for SACS.*

*The desire of this large research university to initiate inquiry-guided
learning experiences more intentionally and earlier in the curriculum led to the engagement of faculty and students in the implementation of a systematic process for accomplishing this goal.*

The Power of Inquiry as a Way of Learning in Undergraduate Education at a Large Research University

*Debra A. Fowler, Pamela R. Matthews, Jane F. Schielack,
Robert C. Webb, X. Ben Wu*

Inquiry-guided learning is not new to our large research-extensive institution (a research university with very high research activity). The ideas of
asking questions and seeking answers have always been associated at our
university with both learning and discovery. In this chapter we present
how, as a natural extension, Texas A&M University infuses inquiry-guided
learning (IGL) more broadly and earlier in the undergraduate learning
experience across multiple disciplines.

As the world becomes increasingly overwhelmed by instant access to
facts and opinions, a scholarly approach to inquiry creates both opportunity and challenges for university education. How might a large research
institution define IGL? For the purposes of this chapter, we consider IGL
comprising the following components: asking questions that are grounded
in an articulated conceptual framework, selecting methods for answering
questions that are appropriate to the discipline, collecting and analyzing
information to answer the questions, linking evidence to explanation, and
communicating valid conclusions.

Texas A&M University is a large, dynamic, diverse, and complex institution with a proud heritage of adapting to the changing needs of its students and their learning. The university's mission statement makes clear
the significance of discovery through inquiry: "[Texas A&M's] mission of

NEW DIRECTIONS FOR TEACHING AND LEARNING, no. 129, Spring 2012 © Wiley Periodicals, Inc.
Published online in Wiley Online Library (wileyonlinelibrary.com) • DOI: 10.1002/tl.20009

providing the highest quality undergraduate and graduate programs is inseparable from its mission of developing new understandings through research and creativity." In keeping with this mission, in 2005, then university president Robert Gates convened a task force to investigate ways to further enhance the experience of undergraduates at Texas A&M. The general student learning outcomes identified by this task force against which enhancement was to be measured were master the depth of knowledge required of a discipline, demonstrate critical analysis skills, communicate effectively in writing and speaking, and provide ethical leadership in a global and diverse society.

Further, a subcommittee of the task force focusing on undergraduate research noted that, in their view, expanding the research education and research opportunities for our undergraduates represents a "natural" way of achieving the aforementioned outcomes most effectively.

The undergraduate research committee of the task force recommended the following:

> Make inquiry-guided learning the standard learning paradigm for as many of our undergraduate courses as is practical.
> Create a new class of courses labeled I-courses, for which inquiry-guided learning is a key element.
> Require all undergraduates to take a minimum of six credit hours of I-courses during their undergraduate career.
> Require that all undergraduate degrees have a "summary research experience" option in their junior/senior year either as a capstone course/project, a research intensive experience, or a senior thesis.
> Provide the appropriate level of institutional resources to support this new academic thrust.

Although these recommendations might be viewed by some as revolutionary, the task force saw them more as evolutionary changes of *existing courses*. In fact, many upper-division curricula already include a significant amount of IGL in the form of inquiry experiences, required research hours, or required theses. The upper division, it turns out, is the easy part of the curriculum to address because these courses can take advantage of the fact that students have gained significant foundational knowledge at this point in their academic careers. The real challenge for implementing these recommendations is in the lower-division courses because many of these courses must be developed with the understanding that students will likely have very little discipline-specific knowledge. However, a number of faculty members on our campus are already successfully offering lower-division inquiry-guided courses.

These courses were identified through a university-wide course inventory based on evidence of the following seven characteristics of critical thinking: assimilating facts, recognizing unanswered questions, formulating strategies for seeking answers, designing appropriate investigations, drawing valid conclusions, communicating effectively, and analyzing critically. The following courses met these seven characteristics: a project-based first-year engineering course, a senior English seminar capstone course, a large introductory geography course that includes a unique inquiry-guided project, a marketing course in which students participate in an intense retail competition, a remote sensing course involving research to address issues in renewable natural resources, and a statistics course including real-world applications of statistical techniques. These courses were identified as models that can be adapted to other disciplines provided the necessary resources are available.

As part of the preparations for reaffirmation of regional accreditation, the university engaged in a comprehensive quality enhancement plan (QEP). The midterm report of the QEP recommended that we revise our plan to focus on one theme—inquiry-guided research education of undergraduates—making that a university-wide effort aimed at enhancing our undergraduate learning outcomes. The revised QEP plan was developed in 2006–07 and it outlined a four-step program:

Step 0—Compilation of a List of Existing Inquiry-Guided Courses: This inventory of courses was to include syllabi and any course material necessary to support its classification as an inquiry-guided course.

Step 1—Formulation of Targeted Learning Outcomes: To support this step, the faculty senate along with the provost's office developed a list of targeted learning outcomes that would serve as the basis for this and all other institutional effectiveness activities on campus, using the learning outcomes from the 2006 task force recommendations as a starting point. Using the list of outcomes, each unit was to devise a plan for carrying out a baseline assessment in the list of inquiry-guided courses already being offered to their students. This baseline assessment would then serve as the starting point for future QEP assessment activities in that unit. This assessment was carried out during the fall term of the 2006–07 academic year in order for this information to be used in developing QEP proposals for the 2007–08 academic year.

Step 2—Solicitation of QEP Proposals: In the fall 2006 semester, all colleges and departments were asked to submit QEP proposals aimed at addressing the learning outcomes that the college or department had identified. Having identified the learning outcomes to be addressed, each department or college could develop a proposal that described how it would enhance the education of the students. A centralized funding source was established at the provost's level to support these activities.

Step 3—QEP Assessment and Reporting: In the years following, each academic program was required to design and implement a program assessment to determine how well the programs were meeting their goals and how they planned to sustain these efforts after the QEP program period ended.

Following the QEP recommendations in 2006, each college and the office of student affairs were asked to submit proposals to implement and assess IGL for undergraduates. The following are examples of progress made as recorded in the reports.

Liberal Arts Inquiry-Guided Implementation Process

Initiated by the university-wide QEP process, the College of Liberal Arts (CLA) set out on a three-year journey to incorporate IGL into courses to enhance the undergraduate education curriculum and meet the learning outcomes desired by the university for each undergraduate. The college initially established the following set of goals:

- Include departments' meaningful participation in inquiry-guided education in their annual evaluations by the dean.
- Increase the number and quality of inquiry-guided courses offered in the college during a three-year period.
- Require that all Liberal Arts students entering after a certain date (to be determined) graduate with at least one inquiry-guided course.
- Improve CLA students' responses to questions about critical inquiry skills in reports from the National Survey of Student Engagement (NSSE) (National Advisory Board, 2005), using the 2005 report as a benchmark and comparing CLA students' responses to NSSE responses. The NSSE questions to be used clustered around coursework emphases, specifically memorizing facts, ideas, or methods; analyzing the basic elements of an idea, experience, or theory; synthesizing and organizing ideas, information, or experiences; and making judgments about the value of information, arguments, or methods.

One important assumption was that a flexible framework would be needed to accommodate the wide range of disciplinary and interdisciplinary approaches in the college, which includes social and behavioral sciences, humanities, performing arts, and critical performance studies. An important first question was, What does "inquiry" look like in fields with diverse methodologies for asking discipline-specific questions?

The plan included developing departmental inquiry-guided courses (I-courses) by focusing on four different departments each year for three years. Departments were selected based on the level of their commitment to curricular innovation, familiarity with assessment, and willingness to try something new with undergraduate learning. The I-courses ranged from introductory to majors courses at all levels. The original four departments chosen to implement the I-courses were Communication, English, Political Science, and Sociology.

NEW DIRECTIONS FOR TEACHING AND LEARNING • DOI: 10.1002/tl

Communication chose to focus on how to create the ideal conditions for the best quality I-courses across the department. To this end, a survey that was developed to assess inquiry-guided approaches to student learning incorporated questions from the NSSE, questions relating to the communications courses, questions focused on personality measures, and questions relating to demographics of the students within the courses.

English chose to convert two lower-level multisection courses to an inquiry-guided format designed to enhance critical thinking and research skills. A rubric was developed for each course to assess the extent to which students gained competency in these skills. One corollary intent was to increase students' understanding of what it means to do research in the humanities.

Political Science developed a process to accurately identify and inventory I-courses and chose to develop a continuous process for assessing the learning outcomes related to IGL. A set of inquiry-guided learning outcomes was developed and then used as the basis to develop pre- and postassessment of students. The assessments specifically measured progress toward formulation, testing, and articulation of hypotheses central to research in political science.

Sociology considered alternate teaching methods for applying the critical standards of sociological research to interpret the scientific strengths and weaknesses of mass media reports of social scientific research. The department's aim in this project was to determine whether an inquiry-guided approach facilitated better learning than lecture only and thus to determine the impact of pedagogical techniques.

The College of Liberal Arts concluded that their departmental approach to incorporating inquiry-guided courses and techniques was a success based on the increased number of I-courses in the English department and the ability to identify the conditions for conducting the highest-quality inquiry courses in Communication, Political Science, and Sociology. The Department of Communication now has benchmarking data for IGL characteristics in targeted majors and core courses, Political Science has developed instruments for pre- and posttesting students' progress toward inquiry-guided knowledge and methods, and Sociology better understands the conditions in which inquiry-based learning must be introduced to produce widespread improvement in analytical understanding. Continued encouragement of inquiry-based courses in the college is planned.

College of Science Inquiry-Guided Implementation Process

The College of Science quality enhancement plan council (COSC-QEPC) chose to implement IGL practices by developing a list of inquiry-guided student learning outcomes desired of students graduating in the College of Science as follows: formulating good questions; examining, identifying, and gathering information; analyzing, interpreting, and presenting results; formulating conclusions and selecting the best solution with appropriate justification; and evaluating the worth and importance of the conclusions drawn. The council then created a plan to identify faculty who were implementing at least one of the five desired outcomes.

The COSC-QEPC reviewed the university-wide inquiry-guided course inventory results as well as additional departmental and instructor information to identify two examples of inquiry-guided approaches by faculty in each of the departments of Biology, Mathematics, Physics and Astronomy, and Statistics. The faculty members identified were interviewed to gather further detail of their teaching process, including techniques for duplicating their approach as well as to identify how the students were being assessed to determine achievement of the desired IGL outcomes. The data are being used to provide contexts for designing online asynchronous environments where faculty can explore inquiry-guided approaches, including the design and implementation of tools and techniques for assessing student achievement of the IGL outcomes.

Center for Teaching Excellence Inquiry-Guided Learning Communities

In support of the QEP to implement IGL across the university, the Center for Teaching Excellence offered two faculty professional development learning communities on the topic of IGL. The faculty learning communities brought eight to twelve faculty and graduate students together for twelve weeks, meeting every other week, to discuss IGL resource articles and chapters from *Teaching and Learning Through Inquiry: A Guidebook for Institutions and Instructors,* edited by Virginia Lee (2004). The goal was implementation of IGL techniques in courses that participants were teaching. Discussions centered on definitions of inquiry in the literature as well as those adopted by the university. Faculty members were asked to select IGL techniques appropriate for their courses and disciplines and to devise a plan for implementation. The faculty learning community then served as a sounding board for faculty to discuss their plans as well as share some of the implementation challenges and successes and receive additional feedback. The faculty learning community sessions also included presentations by faculty members who had been identified through the inquiry-guided course inventory.

Information Technology in Science Center for Teaching and Learning

Within the institutional environment created by the university QEP and with direct access to the high-quality faculty and facilities available at a large research institution, Texas A&M was able to obtain funding from the National Science Foundation for the Information Technology in Science

Center for Teaching and Learning (ITS Center). The central objective of the ITS Center was to produce Grade 7–16 science educators who could infuse inquiry into the classroom through the use of information technology. This objective was met by providing an environment that facilitated interactions among scientists, mathematicians, education researchers, and education practitioners to produce and implement examples of inquiry-based learning in various educational settings. The ITS Center summer institutes allowed participants to explore how information technology can be used to teach important scientific concepts and enabled participants to transform their scientific experiences into inquiry-based learning projects and instructional sequences appropriate for learners in the participants' particular instructional environment.

As a result of the interactions among the various individuals within the project teams, the participating university faculty and teaching assistants designed inquiry-based learning experiences for a variety of undergraduate science courses. ITS participants used information technology in the form of models, visualizations, and data analysis tools to explore current scientific issues and problems within many authentic scientific contexts. They designed inquiry-based learning experiences to engage undergraduate students in the exploration of macro and micro living worlds; mathematical modeling and numerical simulation in science; human and ecological risk assessment; molecular visualization of chemical processes and properties of matter; spatial skills for science education; plant genomics and cellular imaging; energy equilibrium, conservation, and conversion in material science; landscape ecology and conservation; a molecular view of the environment; understanding earth's natural processes; sustainable coastal margins; visualizing biodiversity; science and technology at the nanoscale; and the water environment.

Approximately 180 participants, including nearly fifty science, technology, engineering, and math graduate students and over sixty university faculty, completed two years of activities with the ITS Center. Participants in all cohorts designed and implemented inquiry-based learning experiences and classroom research projects to meet the central objective of their ITS Center learning experience. In terms of distributed expertise, the faculty and graduate students from science disciplines made important contributions to the ITS Center project. Reciprocally, as a result of participation in the ITS Center, university faculty and graduate students grew in their design and implementation of inquiry-based learning. Evidence from graduate students in the sciences showed that, as a result of ITS Center participation, their understanding of the nature of science was enhanced, their skills in the use of information technology and overall skills as scientists were improved, and their knowledge and understanding of science education research had increased (Sell, Peschel, Simmons, and Herbert, 2005). Data collected as part of the ITS Center's evaluation plan showed that science faculty reported a change in attitude through a new appreciation of inquiry-based learning and a desire and interest to incorporate it into their classrooms (McNeal and Anderson, forthcoming).

Institutionalizing Inquiry-Guided Learning

Building on the momentum created by the QEP, two significant university strategic planning processes—the task force on enhancing the undergraduate experience in 2006 and the academic master plan and the teaching and learning roadmap committee in 2009—recommended curriculum development that emphasizes high-impact practices focusing on IGL. These recommendations made IGL an institutional expectation that directly connected to the expectations of the associated agencies responsible for Texas A&M University's accreditation review.

To meet this institutional expectation, a series of programs has been developed or strengthened to broadly and effectively integrate IGL into our curricula. A vibrant and diverse first-year seminar program focusing on IGL has been implemented and is expanding. Capstone courses that focus on inquiry, critical thinking, and integration are being developed or strengthened in most majors. A competitive grant program has been set up by the office of the associate provost for undergraduate studies that will support faculty innovations in curriculum development and course redesign that focus on research-based high-impact practices (Kuh, 2008; Brownell and Swaner, 2010) such as IGL.

A support structure is also being built to support faculty and departmental efforts in their reform and innovations. As part of the implementation of the academic master plan, a Web-based faculty teaching and learning portal is being developed to support faculty efforts to implement high-impact practices including IGL by providing high-quality resources, blended faculty development programs, faculty learning community support, and showcasing of faculty innovation in teaching and learning. A task force on faculty performance evaluation has also been formed as directed by the academic master plan. The committee on teaching performance evaluation convened by the task force recommended summative peer-evaluation programs that build high-impact practices into the reward system as well as a formative peer-mentoring program to help faculty develop these skills. The Center for Teaching Excellence has also started a focus program to support individual departments in their comprehensive curriculum redesign processes, starting with meaningful assessment and articulation of program learning outcomes and ending with the design of programs and courses aligned with the learning outcomes and focusing on high-impact practices including IGL.

Conclusion

For research universities like ours, IGL has long been a critical component of graduate studies as well as a means of offering primarily upper-division

NEW DIRECTIONS FOR TEACHING AND LEARNING • DOI: 10.1002/tl

undergraduates an opportunity to learn and master critical thinking and analytical and communications skills. Our experiences suggest that creating instructional expectations can facilitate the development of programs and supporting structure that also include IGL at all levels through implementation of high-impact practices.

Given the complexity of research universities, a flexible approach is needed to promote IGL to unleash the creativity of the faculty and academic units in developing innovative inquiry-guided learning practices that fit the diverse needs of the disciplinary cultures and their students. Grant-based projects have high potential as those are the hallmark of academic work in research universities and can provide strong incentives for faculty members to engage in these innovations. Collaboration among faculty across various disciplines can be exceptionally productive and lead to sustained efforts and culture-changing impact in academic units.

We are not suggesting that this approach is without its challenges. Implementing any widespread change throughout a curriculum as large as ours and in a research institution as decentralized as ours is difficult, and encouraging IGL has been no different. Although research institutions are the perfect setting for developing and implementing IGL in courses, institutions like ours also face the likelihood that any such initiative is likely to be largely college based. This results in a heavy dependence upon others and the probability of many different models and approaches. This variety can be stimulating but it also makes institutional-level assessment—not to mention curricular coherence—particularly challenging.

In fact, most of the assessments of the IGL initiative were at the program rather than institution level. University-wide early assessments indicated a need for more IGL and later assessments of the process of implementation itself ensured careful tracking and reporting. Assessments of IGL itself, however, occurred in the colleges and departments that participated. One of the lessons we learned for continuing to encourage IGL and developing future initiatives is to build support for the collaborations that facilitate broader institutional commitments and the high-level assessments and other structural foundations that result from those commitments. To require IGL as part of all students' degree plans, for example, processes that must be in place include integrating the courses into existing degree plans, indicating which sections meet the requirement, and facilitating the advising that provides students with the information they need to comply. Future initiatives need to anticipate and develop these support processes as part of the implementation.

In 1998 the Boyer Commission issued recommendations for improving undergraduate education, urging the adoption of IGL as their primary finding. Since the time of Boyer's report the work of George Kuh and others has consistently demonstrated that inquiry-guided approaches, like other integrative approaches, help students develop the deep-thinking skills necessary for successful academic careers. The broad adoption of IGL aligns with our university's mission and is an effective way to enrich undergraduate studies. Early results confirm that IGL can be integrated into all disciplines. Undergraduate students who master the skills and processes involved in inquiry-based learning will not only have an enhanced educational experience, but will also apply these skills in many ways throughout their lives.

References

Brownell, J. E., and L. E. Swaner. *Five High-Impact Practices: Research on Learning Outcomes, Completion, and Quality.* Washington, D.C.: Association of American Colleges and Universities, 2010.

Kuh, G. D. *High-Impact Educational Practices: What They Are, Who Has Access to Them, and Why They Matter.* Washington, D.C.: Association of American Colleges and Universities, 2008.

Lee, V. S., ed. *Teaching and Learning Through Inquiry: A Guidebook for Institutions and Instructors.* Sterling, Va.: Stylus, 2004.

McNeal, K., and R. Anderson. "Adaptation and Development of ITS Learning Ecology Participants." In J. Schielack and S. Knight (eds.), *An Information Technology-based Learning Ecology Model to Promote Science Education Leadership,* forthcoming.

National Advisory Board. *National Survey of Student Engagement.* Bloomington: Center for Postsecondary Research, Indiana University, 2005. Retrieved February 15, 2011, from http://nsse.iub.edu/pdf/NSSE2005_annual_report.pdf.

Sell, K. S., J. Peschel, M. Simmons, and B. Herbert. "IT-Supported Authentic Inquiry in Undergraduate Science and Engineering Education." American Geophysical Union Fall Meeting, Section ED-53A, San Francisco, December 5–9, *Eos, Transactions, American Geophysical Union,* 2005, 86(52), Fall Meet. Suppl., Abstract ED53A-0334.

DEBRA A. FOWLER *is associate director of the Center for Teaching Excellence and visiting assistant professor in the Department of Educational Administration and Human Resource Development at Texas A&M University.*

PAMELA R. MATTHEWS *is associate provost for undergraduate studies and professor in the Department of English at Texas A&M University.*

JANE F. SCHIELACK *is associate dean and professor in the Department of Mathematics at Texas A&M University.*

NEW DIRECTIONS FOR TEACHING AND LEARNING • DOI: 10.1002/tl

ROBERT C. WEBB *is professor in the Department of Physics and Astronomy of Texas A&M University.*

X. BEN WU *is associate dean of faculties, director of the Center for Teaching Excellence, and professor in the Department of Ecosystem Science and Management at Texas A&M University.*

9

Over the past thirty years, inquiry-guided learning has flourished at McMaster University. In this chapter, we discuss some of the enabling factors that helped to encourage early experimentation in inquiry-guided learning and push it toward greater institutionalization as well as some of the challenges and obstacles that had to be overcome.

Lessons Learned: The McMaster Inquiry Story from Innovation to Institutionalization

Carl Cuneo, Del Harnish, Dale Roy, Susan Vajoczki

There are unique moments in curriculum development when an opportunity for a fresh start or a major turn in design fleetingly presents itself. These moments opened up in different locations across McMaster University at different times and eventually led to several quite different initiatives in inquiry-guided learning (IGL). Well-travelled pedagogical ideas combined with administrative openings and faculty interest to foster IGL within and across disciplines. Bell's work on general education (Bell, 1966), along with the ideas of self-directed learning described by Knowles (1975) and Candy (1991), were influential during the early stages of IGL. Pockets of experimentation in collaborative self-directed learning emerged across the campus over a thirty-year period. An institutional culture that prized risk taking and innovation nurtured these experiments.

But innovation does not occur in a vacuum. Traditional teaching methods that emphasized disciplinary content, along with a reward system that emphasized research over teaching, posed significant challenges. And administrators had to be convinced that it was worthwhile to allocate budget items to ill-defined pedagogical initiatives. In this chapter, we discuss some of the enabling factors that helped to encourage early experimentation in IGL and push it toward greater institutionalization, as well as some of the challenges and obstacles that had to be overcome (see Figure 9.1). Although higher education institutions are diverse, each with their unique

New Directions for Teaching and Learning, no. 129, Spring 2012 © Wiley Periodicals, Inc.
Published online in Wiley Online Library (wileyonlinelibrary.com) • DOI: 10.1002/tl.20010

Figure 9.1. Enablers and Challenges to Institutionalization of Inquiry-Guided Learning at McMaster University

Enablers	←————————————→	Challenges
• Innovative institutional culture		• Teaching of fixed disciplinary content
• Diversity in location	**Creation,**	• Instructor turnover
• Open exploration of interdisciplinary content	**development, and**	• Administrator turnover and ignorance
	institutionalization of	
• Student curiosity	**inquiry-guided learning**	• Faculty workload
• Champions of inquiry		• Departmental control of teaching
• Ill-defined inquiry		• Disciplinary boundaries
• Teaching and learning center support		

histories, experiences, and identities, the experience at McMaster University may be useful to other institutions as they experiment with IGL in their own curricula.

Institutional Culture

A university's institutional culture can enable IGL if it values teaching and learning as well as experimentation, creativity, and innovation. In its mission statement, McMaster states that it encourages risk taking on the road to innovation. In fact, most research-intensive universities would say that they value risk taking, creativity, and innovation. What is distinctive about McMaster University is that national surveys of Canadian universities have ranked it as a leader in innovation among Canadian postsecondary universities for many years.

McMaster's focus on innovation has been primarily in the areas of both research and teaching. The teaching of research skills in innovative ways has become a hallmark of its institutional culture. Problem-based learning in medicine successfully integrated itself into this culture. It remained a challenge for IGL to do likewise. The fact that it teaches students the skill of asking research questions and then pursuing and evaluating their own answers through evidence seemed to facilitate its integration into the university's institutional culture. Yet the degree of institutionalization of IGL varies among faculties, departments, programs, and courses across the campus.

Academic Disciplines and Inquiry-Guided Learning

The content of knowledge and research increasingly divides itself into disciplines whose boundaries are closely guarded by university departments and programs and by professional associations representing teachers and researchers. IGL rests on the ever-changing synthesis of skills and disciplinary content. Students learn the skill of asking research questions, not in a disciplinary vacuum, nor within strict disciplinary boundaries, but within the context of "triggers" (that is, course themes). The open-ended exploration of what students need to know to answer their questions is an enabler of IGL. It is an enabler because inquiry skills can cross disciplinary boundaries; instructors can facilitate, and students can engage in, IGL by drawing on specific disciplinary specializations located in diverse departments and programs. Inquiry can never be imposed homogeneously from the center of an institution, but should be nurtured within and across disciplinary boundaries. Thus, IGL resides in many places at McMaster, which has nurtured its growth. Historically, it originated and has been nurtured in three disciplinary locations: within specialized departments and programs, across departments and programs that draw on the synthetic strength of an interdisciplinary approach, and as experiments within individual courses or components of courses.

First, McMaster University became an early pioneer in problem-based learning (PBL), which began in Health Sciences during the early 1970s with the intent of educating future physicians (Barrows and Tamblyn, 1980; Albanese and Mitchell, 1993). The focus was on professional practice and disciplinary specialization. Given the rapid change in medical practice, doctors needed to be lifelong learners. Thus, they needed to learn, not by rote, but by problem-based learning that developed the skills for lifelong learning. The success of PBL (locally and globally) created a positive environment at McMaster University for additional experimentation in teaching and learning. Although there are similarities and differences between problem-based learning and inquiry-based learning (Hudspith and Jenkins, 2001), the similarities became the springboard for experimentation in teaching and learning around IGL at McMaster.

Second, in 1981 McMaster created the elite Arts and Science program that focused on learning through inquiry in an interdisciplinary context that tied together, for example, math and music (Hudspith and Jenkins, 2001; Jenkins, 2007). The intention was to ensure that students had the skills necessary to formulate and answer their own questions and the capacity to become lively, effective citizens. To gain admission to this program students not only had to earn secondary school grades in excess of 90 percent; they were required to complete supplementary applications that described their backgrounds more holistically.

Third, McMaster University followed this early innovation by creating, starting in 1993, several new interdisciplinary and inquiry-based theme schools, such as those in Engineering (for example, Science, Technology and Public Policy) and the Humanities and Social Sciences (for example, International Justice and Human Rights). According to the McMaster University calendar (1999–2000, 128), "[a] Theme School is a centre of interdisciplinary learning in which a group of faculty members identifies a set of intellectual problems arising out of their research, establishes a program of study focused on these problems, and gathers a group of students interested in learning about these problems. Students and faculty will form an intellectual community that will explore these problems through self-directed learning and independent study." These theme schools also appealed to academically gifted undergraduate students, but unlike the Arts and Science program, purposely had a life span of five years.

Fourth, instructors and administrators next turned to the creation of inquiry on a broader basis. In 1998, introductory and interdisciplinary inquiry courses were fashioned at the first-year undergraduate level within each of the Faculties of Sciences, Social Sciences, and Humanities (Roy, 2007). Students merely had to meet their faculty entrance qualifications to enroll in these first-year inquiry courses. In each faculty, instructors collaborated across several departments and disciplines to create and run these courses in several sections, each with no more than twenty-five to thirty students (Cuneo and others, 2001a).

Fifth, in 2000 the university established a new inquiry-based bachelor of health sciences degree that institutionalized inquiry across a wide variety of courses from levels I to IV. Students learn how to apply inquiry skills to a wide variety of health issues. They learn how to ask, reflect, and reformulate questions; how to identify what needs to be known to answer their questions; how to obtain and evaluate information to reflect on evolving questions; how to communicate and work with their peers; and how to self-evaluate their own learning. Interdisciplinarity is a strength of the program. After more than a decade, this program has staying power, buttressed by a dedicated team of instructors and students (Barrett, 2005; Ai, 2008).

Sixth, instructors embedded IGL in individual courses inside programs and departments. In some instances, entire courses were reorganized around IGL (for example, chemistry, mathematics); in other cases, some principles of IGL were adopted (for example, year one biology and environmental sciences; year four sociology).

In all six initiatives, disciplinary and interdisciplinary content has become the vehicle for IGL. But disciplines embedded in departments and programs can also play an obstructionist role and become a challenge to overcome. Programs and departments are the local guardians of professional socialization into the "official knowledge base" of an academic or professional discipline. Content is often "king," relegating learning skills to a secondary handmaiden role. Where programs and departments also control the allocation of teaching responsibilities, disciplinary boundaries often pose a difficult hurdle for inquiry to cross.

Each year the required factual learning grows, particularly in professional disciplines. Failure to teach these facts, it is often argued, puts students at risk. The introduction of a form of learning, inquiry, in which disciplinary knowledge is secondary runs counter to the belief of disciplinary knowledge being paramount (Roy, 2007). Requirements of some professional schools perpetuate the influence of disciplinary knowledge at the expense of inquiry learning. Many faculty believe that students must spend several years acquiring discipline-based knowledge before they can engage in inquiry. There is no doubt that the development of inquiry skills takes both faculty and students time and effort, which is then not available for the traditional content of the discipline. Tensions existed and continue to exist as to where in the curriculum inquiry should reside and the proper balance between content and inquiry skills in inquiry courses (Vajoczki, Watt, Vine, and Liao, 2011).

Students

Students can become the greatest enablers of IGL. At McMaster University, students who are flexible and inquisitive in their approaches to learning and have secondary school learning experiences in inquiry, have often become advocates for IGL. The best advocates are students who recently completed an inquiry-based course and who use what they learned in subsequent courses. They can function as role models: they provide the best evidence that the course works (both for current students and for new and inexperienced faculty) and can provide everyone with honest feedback about what is working and what is not. In our Bachelor of Health Sciences program, students collectively examined their own experiences in IGL and produced a book to tell their story (Ai, 2008). In some inquiry courses, students leave their pool of new inquiry questions for future students. The voices of students who have taken IGL have become enablers that contribute to embedding inquiry within the culture of the institution.

On the other hand, students can pose a challenge to successfully embedding inquiry in the university curriculum. Students who focus on credentialism and exhibit a desire to maximize their progression through the system with minimal effort often find an inquiry learning experience unsettling to their way of thinking and doing. Students who habitually engage in surface learning and rote memory, or engage in plagiarism, have little patience with the time required in critical thinking and reflection. Often students find inquiry daunting initially, because of the disruption to their traditional approaches to teaching and learning (Roy, 2007). However, even within the confines of a single inquiry course, how students view inquiry can evolve. The strong emphasis on peer learning in inquiry creates opportunities for academically challenged students to learn from their more academically gifted peers. Thus, student challenges to embedding and sustaining inquiry within a university culture can often be turned into enablers, depending on the design decisions taken by instructors.

Instructors

University professors and instructors play a critical role in the introduction, development, and sustainment of any pedagogical innovation and can become strong enablers of IGL. At the same time, they can play an obstructionist role that makes the institutionalization of inquiry difficult.

Those who initially find themselves teaching inquiry-based courses are often unfamiliar with the role of a university professor as facilitator rather than lecturer. Many of our university instructors rarely teach first-year undergraduate classes with fewer than several hundred students; in inquiry, they now face the prospect of facilitating a small class of twenty to thirty students. Instructors need an opportunity to experiment with this new role in a supportive environment (Mauer, 2007; Vajoczki, Watt, and Vine, forthcoming).

It was important that our instructors started without a rigid model of inquiry imposed externally. The absence of a prescribed definition made it possible for instructors to actively work out their own definition in practice guided by the wise counsel of the Centre for Leadership in Learning. This built a much more powerful sense of ownership over the results, and, as a bonus, better reflected the core concept of inquiry than a formulaic approach might have. The challenge was to keep the definition from calcifying over time. Inquiry courses worked best when instructors maintained an open mind about the goals of inquiry and what could be accomplished in a single course or a program organized on inquiry principles (Roy, 2007).

In many cases, professors organized themselves into interdisciplinary teams to offer a single inquiry course in multiple sections. The teams would meet regularly to investigate their pedagogy together, to learn from one another's efforts, and to share successes and failures (Cuneo and others, 2001a). Group members explained their experience to colleagues both informally and more formally through papers, seminars, and workshops. The groups have been supported by an educational consultant from the Centre for Leadership in Learning who brought and provided alternatives when the group became stuck (Roy, 2007). To be successful in establishing IGL within the institution's infrastructure, we required a collaborative core of committed, hard-working, and dedicated instructors who were willing to create, think, risk, and implement an inquiry approach as part of a team, and who were prepared to learn a new pedagogical approach. Professors who are teaching oriented or who are bored with their own current approach to teaching have often been early adopters and advocates for IGL. Building on and valuing the knowledge and experience of one another through regular inquiry instructor team meetings contributes to an easier transition to inquiry teaching. But collaborative teamwork among inquiry instructors varied among different sectors of the university. Where it was lacking, inquiry instructors found it more difficult to share inquiry teaching experiences with one another, thereby weakening the enabling potential of instructors.

Yet university professors and instructors can pose some of the greatest obstacles to creating and sustaining IGL in the curriculum. IGL teaches students how to become budding researchers through asking research questions, seeking out what they need to know to answer their questions, evaluating both their questions and their evidence, sharing their discoveries with their peers, and continually reassessing their own learning. Ironically, despite the Boyer Commission on Educating Undergraduates in the Research University (1998), some well-established tenured researchers have been the most resistant to passing on such research skills in an inquiry format. One of their objections is that it takes considerably more time than lecturing on fixed content from the stage, a refrain consistent with "discipline emphasis" previously discussed. One problem rests in the reward system of postsecondary research intensive universities: professors are hired to teach but are granted tenure and promoted primarily on their research publications, regardless of official rules of tenure and promotion. Even though inquiry embodies the integration of research and teaching, it does take time away from the exclusive attention to the research of professors with an eyeball on the list of publications in their CVs. Inquiry requires time-consuming feedback and interaction with students, a fundamental principle of undergraduate education (Chickering and Gamson, 1987), but a process in which not all professors are willing to invest.

Professors' unwillingness to make the investment of time required by IGL may be one of the reasons why some of our interdisciplinary inquiry courses have gone begging for full-time tenured professors as instructors. In some of our divisions, we have had to turn to temporary part-time contract instructors, often on a short-term basis, to staff our inquiry courses.

NEW DIRECTIONS FOR TEACHING AND LEARNING • DOI: 10.1002/tl

They may be graduate students seeking to supplement their income to complete their doctorates; or they may be recently minted doctorates unable to secure a tenure-track position in a university system that relies increasingly on nontenured contract professors. Such temporary contract instructors are often enthusiastic teachers, willing to learn the art of teaching inquiry; many are superior to tenured teachers. But the instability caused by an almost annual turnover in such contract teaching makes it difficult to develop a stable pool of experienced inquiry instructors and provides an important challenge to institutionalizing IGL in the curriculum. In other areas of campus, there has been tremendous success using a permanent and older group of contract instructors over successive years. The key to success in using part-time contract instructors is a stable pool of experienced inquiry instructors from year to year.

Institutionalizing inquiry learning has been difficult. It is hard to sustain and refine a course with faculty assigned to teach inquiry courses on a yearly basis. We tried a variety of models to address high faculty turnover. In the one-year renewable assignment model, a fixed team of the same faculty stayed together for the duration of the course as offered. Another model was the three-year assignment in which professors committed to teaching the course for three successive years. In the first year the instructor was a "novice" and would learn from the more experienced second- and third-year instructors; when instructors entered their second and third year, they would provide mentoring to the "new instructors." This model appeared to work well as it allowed instructors who were new to inquiry to learn and succeed with the new pedagogy before moving on and allowing others an opportunity. Many professors who moved on then became advocates for inquiry in their home departments (Roy, 2007).

Administrators

Senior administrators, with discretionary control over budgets, can become crucial enablers of IGL in the initial, developing, and institutionalizing phases (Justice and others, 2009), but can just as easily pose important challenges to inquiry. Administrators change frequently, and each administrator brings somewhat different skill sets, experiences, and priorities to the table. Further their priorities may shift while in office. We were blessed with a vice president who had tried to teach using inquiry at the fourth-year undergraduate level and who saw immediately the need to start building inquiry skills earlier in the curriculum. Initially, three key deans understood the goals of inquiry well enough to support it; two taught a section of the year-one inquiry course, and all provided funds and support. However, high levels of administrator turnover, combined with a lack of awareness about IGL, differing curriculum priorities, and a developing chasm between administrators and faculty have all posed significant challenges to continuing administrative support for IGL.

NEW DIRECTIONS FOR TEACHING AND LEARNING • DOI: 10.1002/tl

Inquiry champions who are able to demonstrate and communicate to senior administrators the effectiveness of IGL through formative and summative evaluation can help to meet some of these challenges. Evidence of positive learning outcomes (Cuneo and others, 2001b; Trim, 2006; Justice and others, 2007; Justice, Rice, Warry, and Laurie, 2007) and external validation through awards have been effective in securing support with senior administration. Both the first-year interdisciplinary Social Sciences inquiry course and the Bachelor of Health Sciences inquiry program have been recognized internally with the President's Award and externally with the Alan Blizzard Award adjudicated by the Society for Teaching and Learning in Higher Education (Justice and others, 2002; Barrett, 2005). In addition, timing the communication about the benefits of IGL with the introduction of new senior administrators is crucial. In an environment that invites innovation, sometimes successful innovations like IGL are neglected in favor of newer learning innovations.

Champions

Program champions are always enablers of IGL, often in the early stages, though their success in moving initiatives to full-stage institutionalization varies across the campus. Whether the champion is a person, an instructor, a team of instructors, a support unit (such as the Centre for Leadership in Learning), or an administrator, a long-term vision for the program helps, as does a long-term commitment to making it happen and to refining it once it has begun. Most people in the institution have multiple and changing demands on their time, whereas substantial change in institutional practice requires focus and persistence. A few determined individuals can make all the difference.

The role of a program champion has been critical in all of the McMaster variations of incorporating inquiry learning. The informal leadership of the individual champion has been an inspiration to others, but individuals can also burn out without support mechanisms. As a result, institutionalization of IGL has been better served by the collective champion, such as the Bachelor of Health Sciences. There a group of dedicated faculty met often for breakfast, shared experiences, and strategized what became an award-winning honors bachelor degree with a suite of inquiry courses focused on a wide variety of health issues (Barrett and others, 2005). A team champion drawn from seasoned professors from different departments and disciplines led the first-year interdisciplinary inquiry course in the Faculty of Social Sciences (Cuneo and others, 2001a; Roy, 2007). These instructors met regularly, used a common course outline, often used common activities and assignments within their classes, and provided mentorship and moral support to one another (Justice and others, 2002; Inglis and others, 2004). The difference was the lack of an institutionalization of a suite of inquiry courses in the Faculty of Social Sciences from Levels I to IV tied to an undergraduate degree.

Across the campus, Centre for Leadership in Learning staff played the dual role of championing inquiry while at the same time providing logistical support for other champions in faculties, departments, and programs. They were able to provide support for teams of instructors in a variety of forms: recruitment of new team members, insights from others who were further along the path, optional explanations of specific teaching and learning events, recruitment and training of peer tutors, specific feedback to individual instructors, workshops and discussions on relevant topics, and encouragement and moral support (Roy, 2007).

Conclusion

Over the past thirty years IGL has flourished at McMaster University, but always in a tension between enabling and challenging conditions. Lack of succession planning, changeover of administrators, faculty control of budgets, departmental control of teaching resources, instructor burnout associated with teaching inquiry, and current budget constraints have all challenged the institutionalization of IGL in our curriculum. By contrast, important enabling conditions include administrators with a clear understanding of inquiry; succession planning of inquiry instructors; and collaboration among instructors, who together provide optimal conditions for students to ask questions, to seek what they need to know in ways determined by themselves, and to constantly reevaluate what they found. These conditions set the stage for successful, lifelong inquiry learning.

References

Ai, R. *Choose Your Own Inquiry!* Lanham, Md.: University Press of America, 2008.

Albanese, M. A., and S. Mitchell. "Problem-based Learning—A Review of Literature on its Outcomes and Implementation Issues." *Academic Medicine*, 1993, 68(1), 52–81.

Barrett, S. *Skills Development with Students and Explicit Integration Across Four Years of the Curriculum.* The Alan Blizzard Award Paper, Special Publication of the Society for Teaching and Learning in Higher Education, Toronto, 2005.

Barrows, H., and R. M. Tamblyn. *Problem-based Learning: An Approach to Medical Education.* New York: Springer, 1980.

Bell, D. *The Reforming of General Education.* New York: Columbia University Press, 1966.

Boyer Commission on Educating Undergraduates in the Research University. *Reinventing Undergraduate Education. A Blueprint for America's Research Universities.* Stony Brook: State University of New York, 1998. Retrieved February 10, 2011, from http://naples.cc.sunysb.edu/Pres/boyer.nsf/.

Candy, P. *Self-Direction for Lifelong Learning.* San Francisco: Jossey-Bass, 1991.

Chickering, A. W., and Z. F. Gamson. "Seven Principles for Good Practice in Undergraduate Education." *American Association for Higher Education Bulletin*, 1987, 39(7), 3–7. Retrieved February 10, 2011, from http://www.aahea.org/bulletins/articles/sevenprinciples1987.htm.

Cuneo, C., and others. "Thinking and Doing 'Outside the Box': Interdisciplinary Inquiry Learning Partnerships." *Research and Development in Higher Education,* 2001a, *24,* 15–22.

Cuneo, C., and others. "Critical Thinking Under Pressure: Does Inquiry Make a Difference?" Paper delivered at 21st Annual Conference of the Society for Teaching and Learning in Higher Education, Memorial University, St. Johns, Newfoundland, 2001b.

Hudspith, B., and H. Jenkins. *Teaching and the Art of Inquiry.* Green Guide No. 3. Halifax, Nova Scotia: Society for Teaching and Learning in Higher Education, 2001.

Inglis, S., and others. "Cross-cultural Simulation to Advance Student Inquiry." *Simulation & Gaming: An Interdisciplinary Journal of Theory, Practice and Research,* 2004, *35*(4), 476–487.

Jenkins, H. "The Origins of Inquiry in McMaster's Arts and Science Program." In C. Knapper (ed.), *Proceedings from Experiences with Inquiry Learning.* Hamilton, Ontario: McMaster University, 2007.

Justice, C., and others. *A Grammar for Inquiry: Linking Goals and Methods in a Collaboratively Taught Social Sciences Inquiry Course.* The Alan Blizzard Award Paper, Special Publication of the Society for Teaching and Learning in Higher Education, Toronto, 2002.

Justice, C., and others. "Inquiry in Higher Education: Reflections and Directions on Course Design and Teaching Methods." *Innovative Higher Education,* 2007, *31*(4), 201–214.

Justice, C., J. Rice, W. Warry, and I. Laurie. "Taking an 'Inquiry' Course Makes a Difference: A Comparative Analysis of Student Learning." *Journal on Excellence in College Teaching,* 2007, *18*(1), 57–77.

Justice, C., and others. "Inquiry-based Learning in Higher Education: Administrators' Perspectives on Integrating Inquiry Pedagogy into the Curriculum." *Higher Education,* 2009, *58,* 841–855.

Knowles, M. *Self-Directed Learning.* Upper Saddle River, N.J.: Prentice Hall, 1975.

Mauer, D. "Teaching Inquiry at McMaster: The Impact on the Instructor." In C. Knapper (ed.), *Experiences with Inquiry Learning: Proceedings of a Symposium at McMaster University.* Hamilton, Ontario: Centre for Leadership in Learning, McMaster University, 2007.

McMaster University. *Undergraduate Calendar.* 1999–2000. Retrieved February 10, 2011, from http://registrar.mcmaster.ca/CALENDAR/PDF-Archive/McMaster_UG_Calendar -1999-2000web.pdf.

Roy, D. "Weaving Inquiry into the First-Year Experience: A Rope of Sand." In C. Knapper (ed.), *Proceedings from Experiences with Inquiry Learning.* Hamilton, Ontario: McMaster University, 2007.

Trim, K. *Developing Inquiry Skills with Undergraduate Students at McMaster 1999–2004: Ongoing Formative and Summative Evaluation for the Faculties of Science and Health Science.* Unpublished PhD dissertation. Hamilton, Ontario: McMaster University, 2006.

Vajoczki, S., S. Watt, and M. M. Vine. "Inquiry Learning: Instructor Perspectives." *Canadian Journal for the Scholarship of Teaching and Learning,* forthcoming.

Vajoczki, S., S. Watt, M. M. Vine, and X. R. Liao. "Inquiry Learning: Level, Discipline, Class Size, What Matters?" *International Journal for the Scholarship of Teaching and Learning,* 2011, *5*(1).

CARL CUNEO *was part of an interdisciplinary team of instructors that founded an award-winning inquiry course design for entering university students in the Faculty of Social Sciences at McMaster University in 1998. Although officially retired from the Department of Sociology since 2008, as professor emeritus he has continued to teach inquiry by exploring with his students the synergies between inquiry, social media, and mobile technologies.*

DEL HARNISH *is a 3M fellow and Bachelor of Health Sciences program dean. He was involved in the development of large course-based inquiry, science inquiry models, and the inquiry-rich health science program. He and Cuneo developed the first interdisciplinary inquiry-based technology platform at McMaster. With Cuneo and Roy, he has invested considerable energy over fifteen years in the discussion of elements of this story.*

DALE ROY *spent more than twenty-five years working at the Centre for Leadership in Learning before retiring in 2008. During that time he coordinated the 3M fellowship program and worked with McMaster faculty on many of the efforts to initiate and institutionalize teaching through inquiry described in this chapter.*

SUSAN VAJOCZKI *is the director of the Centre for Leadership in Learning at McMaster University and an associate professor in the school of Geography & Earth Sciences. She has taught in and provided pedagogical support to the first-year inquiry course in social sciences since 2005 and has incorporated inquiry learning into a number of environmental and earth sciences courses.*

NEW DIRECTIONS FOR TEACHING AND LEARNING • DOI: 10.1002/tl

10

This chapter reviews the eight institutional case studies in this volume and analyzes similarities and differences in their conceptions of inquiry-guided learning, the dynamics of implementation, methods of assessment, and future plans.

Opportunities and Challenges in Institutionalizing Inquiry-Guided Learning in Colleges and Universities

Virginia S. Lee

Inquiry-guided learning (IGL) has widespread appeal in higher education as a suite of teaching strategies that promotes learning through students' increasingly independent investigation of questions, problems, and issues using the methods of inquiry of the disciplines. Framed as especially appropriate for research universities, IGL has been adopted equally by public and private institutions, comprehensive universities, and liberal arts colleges in the United States and abroad. The appeal of IGL is so broad that it provides a unique window into the dynamics of undergraduate reform in higher education: the collective hopes projected onto IGL as a promising mode of learning and the realities of its implementation.

Choosing and Interpreting Inquiry-Guided Learning

The eight institutional case studies in this volume represent a range of institutions of higher education from four countries (see Table 10.1). Despite their diversity, IGL was attractive to all of them for the same and different reasons. In New Zealand the legislature mandated that research institutions bridge their teaching and research missions through a teaching-research nexus. In the United Kingdom the government funded national Centres for Excellence in Teaching and Learning (CETL) as hubs of innovation and dissemination. And in the United States the Southern Association of Colleges and Schools (SACS), the accrediting body of the

NEW DIRECTIONS FOR TEACHING AND LEARNING, no. 129, Spring 2012 © Wiley Periodicals, Inc.
Published online in Wiley Online Library (wileyonlinelibrary.com) • DOI: 10.1002/tl.20011

southeast region, requires a quality enhancement plan (QEP) as part of the reaccreditation process: a carefully designed course of action to address a student learning need on campus. In response to these varied mandates, IGL emerged as the form of institutional response in six of the case studies represented in this volume. For two institutions—McMaster University and Miami University—the choice of IGL was more idiosyncratic, emerging from a top-down "student as scholar" initiative and a commitment to teaching the skills of research across the university, respectively.

For all of these institutions, IGL offered many potentially attractive features: a way of learning consistent with university-level study, inquiry experiences with appropriate support embedded in courses for successful independent research later in the curriculum, the ability to further a range of desired student learning outcomes, consistency with desired attributes of university graduates, and the promise of institutional integrity by bridging the teaching and research missions.

As the institutions move toward implementation, greater distinctions among the institutions emerge related to their interpretation of IGL and where in the curriculum it resides (see Table 10.1). In Chapter One I discussed in detail the unique challenges IGL poses as a suite of teaching practices with no single formula for classroom practice. Consequently, at the outset each institution struggled with the development of a common language for IGL including a set of guidelines for its integration into courses and the curriculum. In doing so they drew upon a wealth of strategies including definitions, student learning outcomes, existing general models (for example, Kolb's experiential learning cycle), newly designed inquiry models (for example, Levy's modes of inquiry), developmental rubrics of key abilities and component inquiry skills, and related constructs such as critical thinking and information literacy. Interestingly, in all cases, beginning efforts to delimit IGL led to generous license in the ultimate interpretation of IGL by faculty members in their courses.

Given the strong academic value of autonomy, differences in disciplinary cultures, and the varied assumptions held by instructors about teaching and learning (see Chapter One), the requirement of flexibility of interpretation is not at all surprising. In this volume there are examples of IGL in a variety of disciplines and levels of study: one-credit first-year seminars, large enrollment gateway courses, courses in the major, capstone courses, and graduate seminars (see Table 10.1). In almost all cases, implementation of IGL at one place in the curriculum leads to wider dissemination elsewhere. For example, Virginia Wesleyan College implemented IGL first in a one-credit first-year seminar in coordination with a campus-wide cocurricular seminar series and information literacy program conducted by the campus library. As instructors became more invested in IGL, they integrated it into more of their courses, spreading it across the curriculum. The college is now transitioning from three- to four-credit courses as a further outgrowth of the initiative.

New Directions for Teaching and Learning • DOI: 10.1002/tl

Table 10.1. Selected Features of IGL in Institutional Case Studies: Part One

Institution/Feature	Type of Institution	Why IGL?	Where Does IGL Reside?	Interpretation of IGL
McMaster University	Research-intensive, Canada	Early success of PBL in medicine Commitment to teaching skills of research across university	PBL in medical school Elite arts and science program Several interdisciplinary and IGL-based theme schools Introductory and interdisciplinary courses Inquiry-based BA in health sciences	Bell work on general education Self-directed learning—Knowles, Candy Left open to interpretation in disciplines
Marymount University	Midsized, independent Catholic, United States	QEP: integrating research across undergraduate (UG) curriculum University mission Students need classroom experiences for successful research	DISCOVER program First-year seminar Transfer seminar Refocused UG curriculum: requires major courses with IGL	Lee definition Hudspith & Jenkins process Justice et al. inquiry outcomes Research skill development framework Left open to interpretation in disciplines
Miami University	Public, comprehensive, United States	Initiated by higher administration "Student as scholar" IGL provides support students need	27 high-enrollment gateway courses Some second- and third-year business courses Expanding to other parts of UG curriculum	Lee definition IGL in different disciplines Inverted classroom Faculty choose model best for them/discipline
New Zealand Universities	Four varied universities, New Zealand	NZ legislative requirement that teaching and research be closely related Tertiary education strategy	Stages 1, 2, and 3 inquiry in 14 subject areas in 4 institutions Focus: large, first-year sociology course and ecology degree program	Spronken-Smith and Walker grounded framework for inquiry approach; Staver and Bay mode of inquiry Levy's model

(continued)

Table 10.1. (Continued)

Institution/Feature	Type of Institution	Why IGL?	Where Does IGL Reside?	Interpretation of IGL
Texas A&M University	Public, research-intensive, United States	Mission statement Task force convened by president Recommendations of UG research subcommittee QEP	Every college First-year seminars Capstone courses	Learning outcomes Critical thinking Relevant NSSE items
University of Gloucestershire	Small university, professional studies, United Kingdom	University strategic plan Award of national CETL status Desired student learning outcomes	Active learning induction Broadcast Journalism Business program development	Kolb Performances for understanding Teaching-research nexus
University of Sheffield	Research-intensive, United Kingdom	Research university; IGL links teaching, research missions University strategic plan Attributes of Sheffield graduate Award of national CETL status	Widely distributed across the curriculum including graduate study	No one way to conceptualize IGL framework Modes of inquiry Role of information literacy
Virginia Wesleyan College	Small, Methodist-affiliated, liberal arts, United States	QEP Helping first-year students transition from high school to college Critical thinking and information literacy	First-year seminar Relating to general studies frames of reference Spreading to entire curriculum Transition from three- to four-credit courses	Lee definition Developed own definition Critical thinking

NEW DIRECTIONS FOR TEACHING AND LEARNING • DOI: 10.1002/tl

Implementing Inquiry-Guided Learning

As the institutions represented in this volume move further into implementation, more differences emerge among them including the faculty development and assessment methods they use (see Table 10.2). In addition to where innovation through IGL resides in the curriculum, from localized instantiations to more widespread integration, certain features are unique to specific institutions. For example, over a thirty-year period, teaching research skills in new ways has become a hallmark of the culture at McMaster University, an early pioneer in problem-based learning, and national surveys recognized the university as a leader in innovation. Virginia Wesleyan College, a small, Methodist-affiliated institution, has coordinated its first-year inquiry seminar with cocurricular events including a campus-wide symposium and the annual commencement address by a prominent person. Marymount University has branded its inquiry-guided learning as the DISCOVER program. The University of Sheffield, as a nationally designated teaching and learning development center, conducts cross-institutional studies; on its own campus it has pioneered inquiry "collaboratories," specially designed classrooms for courses with a strong inquiry component.

Flexibility in the interpretation of IGL by individual instructors in different disciplines and developmental levels (discussed previously and in Chapter One) necessitates ongoing faculty development using a range of methods. In general, most institutions underestimate greatly the importance of faculty development in education reform initiatives, particularly at the outset. Among the institutions in this volume, faculty development takes a variety of forms: workshops using external and internal facilitators, faculty learning communities, specialized support for academic departments and schools, summer institutes, teaching and learning Web portals, and more (see Table 10.2). The methods they select depend upon the nature and size of their institution, the locus of IGL in the curriculum, and the resources available for faculty development. For example, at Virginia Wesleyan College faculty development itself has evolved as an inquiry-driven process over time. McMaster University addressed the reality of instructor turnover in teaching inquiry courses by assigning three-member rotating teams of instructors for given courses; each team comprised members of three-, two-, and one-year tenures, the latter designated the "novice." And at Texas A&M University, the Center for Teaching Excellence initiated a focus program to support academic departments in the development of outcomes and appropriate assessment processes. Along with assessment (discussed next), faculty development was a way of gradually honing the institution's understanding of IGL and enhancing its impact on student learning.

For any reform initiative that involves a conspicuous outlay in resources, whether in the form of time or money, assessment is critical both

Table 10.2. Selected Features of IGL in Institutional Case Studies: Part Two

Institution/ Feature	Uniqueness Regarding Implementation	Faculty Development Issues	Assessment of IGL
McMaster University	30-year initiative National surveys ranked as leader in innovation among Canadian universities Teaching research skills in new ways hallmark of culture Pioneer in PBL in medicine	Important for those who rarely teach first-year students in small classes Three-year assignment with rotating "novice"	Extensive within course, program and longitudinal assessment
Marymount University	DISCOVER program DISCOVER assessment tool	Two days with external consultant Specialized training for four schools Specialized support for DSC 101 Support for conference attendance	Existing instruments: annual alumni survey, NSSE, retention data DISCOVER assessment tool: AACU VALUE rubric, Bowling Green State, Adelaide's RSD Framework Student Inquiry Skills and Attitudes Questionnaire
Miami University	President leadership Implementation in large classes	Varied depending on discipline External consultants by discipline Assistance from internal units Convened cohorts with readings, discussion	Formative assessment Course observations by administrative team Student focus groups End of semester surveys and assessment of student writing using critical thinking rubric Longitudinal study
New Zealand Universities	Cross-institutional study Role of government in stimulating IGL Context of K-12 education	Collaborative team teaching approach	Student survey on perceived higher-order learning outcomes using Bloom's taxonomy

NEW DIRECTIONS FOR TEACHING AND LEARNING • DOI: 10.1002/tl

Institution			
Texas A&M University	Decentralized Identification of existing models to use as models	CTE learning communities ITS Center Summer Institutes Faculty teaching and learning portal CTE focus program	Each program designs own assessment process
University of Gloucestershire	Convergence of university strategic plan, Teaching, Learning, and Assessment Strategic Framework, and national center	Staff development events Consultation with individual staff Business simulation programs Need for flexibility	Student survey of degree of academic challenge and nature of learning experience
University of Sheffield	Government funded program Intra- and interinstitutional development Focus on arts, humanities, social sciences Model development Importance of information literacy Multiprofessional partnerships Student partnerships Inquiry "collaboratories"	IGL champions Formal, informal, and social networking Staff development workshops with experiential focus Dissemination of practice	CETL supported, conducted SoTL and research for IGL "Theory of change" evaluation methodology
Virginia Wesleyan College	Inquiry-guided faculty development Initiative structured around annual big question Coordination with cocurricular	Faculty development as inquiry process Steering committee itself provides workshops Workshops as labs for classrooms Series of workshops led by faculty Web-based archive	Assess development of disposition for college learning Student self-report Students' ability to approach a complex problem in final exam

for the purposes of improving practice (that is, formative) and for making decisions regarding future asset allocation (that is, summative). Arguably the most powerful form of assessment is the direct assessment of student learning using instructor-designed tests and other assignments from which instructors identify patterns of strength and weakness in student mastery of intended knowledge, ability, and value outcomes and the probable relationship of these patterns to instruction. Further, instructors use these patterns of student performance and their relationship to instruction to modify future instruction. Of course, other, less direct forms of assessment have their place as well.

The institutions in this volume used a variety of methods to assess the effectiveness of instruction using IGL (see Table 10.2) including course- and program-based assessment, student and alumni surveys, the National Survey of Student Engagement (NSSE), course observations, student focus groups, longitudinal studies, and interinstitutional research studies. For example, Marymount University developed its own DISCOVER assessment tool, drawing upon existing instruments such as the Association of American Colleges and Universities' VALUE rubrics, Bowling Green State University's Developmental Stages of Inquiry, and the University of Adelaide's Research Skills Development Framework. Several institutions—McMaster University, the New Zealand universities, University of Gloucestershire, and University of Sheffield—have made important contributions to the scholarship of teaching and learning based on their extensive assessment of IGL. Texas A&M University has given programs substantial discretion in designing their own assessment processes.

Challenges in Implementation and Future Plans

Despite their substantial progress implementing IGL, the institutions in this volume also encountered and continue to encounter substantial challenges in implementation (see Table 10.3). This is not at all surprising given widespread institutional inertia in all shapes and guises in the face of reform of any kind including IGL. In fact, the contribution from McMaster University (see Chapter Nine) carefully weighs the challenges and opportunities of implementation over the institution's thirty-year history of integrating IGL at many points in the undergraduate and graduate curriculum. Their experience speaks well for many of the colleges and universities here. And in Chapter One I described the special challenges that IGL as a suite of teaching strategies that defies a simple formula for classroom practice poses as the focus of reform despite its widespread appeal in theory.

Almost all institutions encountered substantial systemic resistance to change in the form of the tenacity of the content-coverage paradigm of teaching; the comparative importance of the research mission, particularly in research universities; the rigidity of disciplinary boundaries; the credentialing requirements of professional programs; the many competing

Table 10.3. Selected Features of IGL in Institutional Case Studies: Part Three

Institution/Feature	Challenges in Implementation	Future Plans
McMaster University	Emphasis on research versus teaching Emphasis on content coverage Disciplinary boundaries Requirements of some professional schools Students who focus on credentialing and getting by IGL takes more time Reward system Turnover in adjunct faculty	
Marymount University	Faculty development for adjuncts Instructor concern about giving up control Uneven adoption by different disciplines Student resistance Decreases in impact of initiative on retention and student self reports Development of assessment tools that faculty support	Longitudinal assessment Development of assessment measures for years two and three
Miami University	Faculty motivation to participate uneven Student resistance initially Importance of administrative support at all levels Challenges in sustaining the initiative Faculty turnover Costs	Non-Top 25 courses starting to embrace IGL Upward integration from first year in Department of Psychology Development of first-year research experience
New Zealand Universities		Possible expansion of IGL in New Zealand universities due to changes in K-12 education

(continued)

Table 10.3. (*Continued*)

Institution/Feature	Challenges in Implementation	Future Plans
Texas A&M University	Bigness and decentralization Institutional-level assessment	Making IGL the standard for as many undergraduate courses as possible Expansion of IGL first-year seminar (FYS) program Development/ strengthening of capstone courses in major Competitive grant program focusing on research-based high-impact practices Development of Web-based portal Reconsideration of faculty evaluation
University of Gloucestershire	Disjuncture between bottom-up and top-down approaches Pressures on staff time Systemic obstacles to change Department managers see initiative as opportunity to get resources Differences in how staff interpret IGL	
University of Sheffield	Tensions between research and teaching Educational development competing with faculty's other commitments Developing accessible, shareable language regarding IGL	Increase in inquiry "collaboratories" Student Ambassadors for Learning and Teaching
Virginia Wesleyan College	Initial faculty resistance to IGL	Fall 2009 motion to move from three- to four-credit course structure Formal linkage of FYS to four-credit courses

responsibilities and tasks for faculty members' time; student resistance to taking greater responsibility for their own learning that IGL demands; and the incentive structure for promotion and tenure that favors research over teaching, particularly in research universities. The growing use of adjunct faculty also poses a special challenge given their focused time commitment to the institutions in which they teach, low pay, and high turnover.

NEW DIRECTIONS FOR TEACHING AND LEARNING • DOI: 10.1002/tl

With some success during the initial stages of implementation, several institutions noted challenges in sustaining IGL over time. Interested faculty members and receptive disciplines and programs typically account for the first flush of success with any reform initiative; later success depends upon convincing the reluctant faculty members and departments that the time and resources required for IGL are worth the effort. In addition, changing course assignments and other forms of faculty turnover require continuous faculty development efforts. Shifting institutional priorities and administrative turnover are other serious challenges. Even among many colleges and universities for which teaching has been a central focus of the mission, the research star is ascending as the research university becomes the aspirational model for more and more institutions of higher learning. Further, a highly placed administrator, generous in support of IGL, may leave, only to be replaced by someone far less supportive of the initiative.

Challenges notwithstanding, several colleges and universities in this volume note a tendency for IGL to spread from its initial locus in the curriculum to other courses and programs over time (see Table 10.3). For example, at Miami University the success of integrating IGL in large-enrollment gateway courses has paved the way for broader dissemination: the Department of Psychology is planning upward integration of IGL in its program, and the university is planning a first-year research experience. And, most dramatically, with initial implementation of IGL in a one-credit first-year seminar the enthusiasm of the faculty at Virginia Wesleyan Colleges for IGL has grown to such an extent that they are moving from a three- to four-credit course structure to enable richer student engagement in all courses. Other institutions are planning refinements in their practice of IGL in the form of better assessment measures, the construction of more classrooms conducive to student inquiry, the greater use of students as ambassadors for IGL, and other faculty development strategies such as grant programs. In addition, our New Zealand colleagues note promising changes in K-12 education there, which should enhance student receptivity to (and even expectation for) IGL at the tertiary level.

Conclusion

Adopted by a wide array of institutions of higher education throughout the world, IGL poses special challenges as a suite of teaching strategies with no single formula for classroom practice. At the same time, the integration of IGL into college and university curricula provides a window into the dynamics of undergraduate reform more generally. In the early stages of implementation, all institutions grapple with IGL's open-endedness and work hard to establish a common language, whether in the form of a definition, related student learning outcomes, or models. Then, paradoxically, as implementation continues, faculty members who have demanded detailed guidance in transforming their courses through IGL ultimately require great flexibility and wide discretion in its interpretation in the context of their disciplines and courses. Faculty development strategies need to adapt to this reality, morphing from traditional workshop offerings that demonstrate "how to do IGL" to faculty learning communities and other peer networks in which instructors share and learn from each others' pitfalls and best practices.

The eight case studies in this volume also remind us through vivid illustration that the successful integration of IGL in the curriculum depends upon the broader institutional context. The embedding of obsolete paradigms of teaching and learning in institutions' thought, practice, and management of space and time; shifting institutional priorities; faculty and administrator turnover; the misalignment of the incentive structure with the trajectory of reform; the credentialing requirements in certain professional programs; budget constraints that lead to larger course enrollments—all institutions must navigate these and other challenges successfully to sustain reform through IGL over time. From the standpoint of student learning and faculty vitality, it is in their best interest to do so.

VIRGINIA S. LEE *is principal and senior consultant of Virginia S. Lee &* *Associates, LLC (Durham, North Carolina), a consulting firm that specializes* *in teaching, learning, and assessment in higher education.*

NEW DIRECTIONS FOR TEACHING AND LEARNING • DOI: 10.1002/tl

INDEX